KENNY EVERETT'S
ULTIMATE
LOO BOOK

KENNY EVERETT'S ULTIMATE LOO BOOK

KENNY EVERETT and SIMON BOOKER

ANGUS & ROBERTSON PUBLISHERS

ANGUS & ROBERTSON PUBLISHERS

16 Golden Square, London W1R 4BN,
United Kingdom,
and Unit 4, Eden Park, 31 Waterloo Road,
North Ryde, NSW, Australia 2113,

First published in the United Kingdom
by Angus & Robertson (UK) in 1988.
First published in Australia
by Angus & Robertson Publishers in 1988.
Reprinted 1988 [twice]

British Library Cataloguing in Publication Data

Everett, Kenny,
    Kenny Everett's ultimate loo book.
    I. Title II. Booker, Simon
    828'.91409

    ISBN 0 207 15849 5

Typeset in Century Schoolbook
by The Word Shop, Rossendale.

Printed in Great Britain
by Richard Clay Ltd, Bungay, Suffolk

Introduction

Hello, darling reader. Now that you are the proud owner of *Kenny Everett's Ultimate Loo Book*, there are a few things you should know about the world's first paperback laxative.

All done in the best possible taste, this *pooh-pourri* has been rigorously tested under laboratory conditions, given a shampoo and set and baked for half an hour in a pre-heated oven.

As you will have guessed by now, this is no ordinary book. It has many other uses – like unblocking drains, swatting wasps and propping up that wobbly leg on the kitchen table.

And this is the first ever bathroom book which – when placed at the correct angle – will change into a life-size model of Ronald Reagan's left knee-cap while playing Beethoven's Fifth Symphony.

If, like me, you've passed countless bathroom hours counting the bristles on your toothbrush or wondering why Bo Derek constantly refuses to return your calls, be of good cheer because *Kenny Everett's Ultimate Loo Book* is here to amaze, astound, educate and delight.

Just think of all that time you spend on the loo. Eleven wasted minutes every day. That's seventy wasted hours every year!

Now, with the help of this magical volume you can put all that behind you . . .

* Find out what the fickle finger of fate has in store with the week's Astro-loogical forecast.
* Learn how to lead a fuller life with help from The Kenny Everett Guide To Survival in the Twentieth Century.
* Dazzle your nears and dears with a string of fascinating facts about stars' birthdays and anniversaries.
* Win a fortnight for two in Claire Rayner's cleavage, or a night out with the brussel sprout of your choice. (Offer not open to residents of the Isle of Man.)

* Develop a brain the size of a bungalow with help from the Bathroom Brain-teasers.
* Enjoy the misery of your fellow human beings as you peruse the heart-rending, tear-jerking, muesli-blending pages of Uncle Ken's Agony Column.
* Improve your lifestyle both in and out of the bathroom with Helpful Household Hints.

And if you enjoy reading this book half as much as I do, then I'll have enjoyed it twice as much as you . . .

January 1st

One of the most useful features of this book is the COMPLETELY AND UTTERLY INFALLIBLE FATE-FORECASTING SERVICE. Thanks to the Zodiac charts (and the tireless efforts of my personal analyst, Sue E. Cidal), I have prepared a weekly **Astro-Loogical** chart, highlighting some of the thrills and spills in store for you.

This week's (fairly) lucky star sign is

A challenging time ahead when you will be faced with many tempting choices, like whether to become an international sex symbol or whether to embark on major dental surgery. If you opt to have all your teeth removed, one highly effective way to fill the cavity is to install a three-piece suite.

January 2nd

Bathroom Brain-teasers

1 Which newspaper does Superman/Clark Kent work for?
2 Why don't actors like to whistle in theatres?
3 Is it true what they say about Dixie?
4 How many 'm's are there in the word 'cornucopia'?
5 How many miles of arteries, capillaries and veins are there in the human body?

(Answers at foot of next page)

Happy Birthday to photographer David Bailey (1938).

American comedienne Phyllis Diller hates having her photograph taken. She says, 'My photographs do me an injustice . . . they look just like me.'

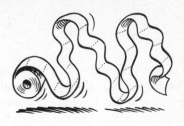

January 3rd

PHILOSOPHICAL STATEMENT OF THE DAY

'I shop – therefore I am.'

Happy Birthday to Danish musician and comedian Victor Borge (1909). A wonderfully witty man, Victor once said, 'Ah, Mozart! He was happily married – but his wife wasn't.'

Today is also the anniversary of the birth of Clement Attlee (British Labour Prime Minister from 1945 to 1951). Old Clem also had a way with words and penned the following poem about himself:

> Few thought he was even a starter
> There were many who thought themselves smarter
> But he ended PM, CH and OM
> An Earl and a Knight of The Garter.

Brain-teaser Answers

1) Daily Planet.   2) Superstition meaning that someone's going to lose a job.   3) Yes, but she never meant to harm the gerbil.
4) Maggie Thatcher's armpit.   5) Sixty thousand miles!

January 4th

Uncle Ken's Agony Column

Because I care enormously about my fellow human beings, I find that many people write to me seeking advice about their personal problems. When all else has failed, when the Agony Aunts are stumped for a solution, people turn to Uncle Ken as a last resort, knowing that I'm utterly trustworthy when it comes to preserving confidentiality. Suckers.

Here's one such letter I received recently:

Dear Uncle Ken...

I am just an ordinary housewife called Brian. My life has been thrown into complete turmoil because I've discovered that my mother is really an airing cupboard. I'm so ashamed about stuffing towels and sheets into a member of my family. What shall I do?

Uncle Ken writes:

Dear Brian,

This is a very common complaint amongst women of your height.

My advice is to tell your mother that she's not really an airing cupboard. Try convincing her that she's a Morphy Richards refrigerator – that way you'll be able to stuff her full of fish fingers instead of towels.

I look forward to receiving your cheque.

Yours until the heavens turn into a side-salad,

Uncle Ken

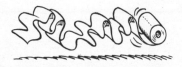

January 5th

Being a fellow member of the human race, I consider it my duty to help others through life whenever possible. In the course of my forty-odd years on this earth, I have accumulated a wealth of knowledge (as well as an endless supply of odd socks). It is therefore with great pride that I proudly present

THE
KENNY EVERETT
GUIDE TO SURVIVAL IN THE
TWENTIETH CENTURY

(and how to avoid getting soup in your shoes)

Part One:
NEVER EAT A HEDGEHOG WITHOUT PEELING IT FIRST

Happy Birthday to His Majesty King Juan Carlos of Spain (born 1938). (I went to Spain once and turned down a paella-spattered invitation to meet His Maj. Let's face it, once you've seen Juan Carlos, you've seen 'em all . . .)

January 6th

Happy Birthday to Rowan 'rubber-face' Atkinson (1955) and Sacha 'knobbly-knees' Distel (1932).

(Score 20 extra points if your knees can hum 'The Blue Danube'.)

Today's Loo Laff

Sales of tea were dropping dramatically, so the advertising agency sent their head honcho to Rome to persuade the Pope to take part in a TV commercial.

'We'll give you half a million, just to say "Give Us This Day Our Daily Tea".'

The Pope shook his head. 'I'm sorry, but I can't do it.'

'A million then,' said the ad-man.

Again, the Pope refused.

'OK,' said the advertising whizz-kid, 'Three million pounds – that's our final offer.'

Still the Pope refused to make the commercial.

Back at his office, the executive reported the failure of his mission. 'I don't understand why he said no. I wonder how much he's getting from the bread people . . .'

January 7th

Bathroom Brain-teasers

1 Which type of TV programme is best for your health?
2 Can you lick the backs of your knees?
3 Name the characters played by George Cole and Dennis Waterman in 'Minder'.
4 Whose turn is it to pay for lunch?
5 Does your chewing-gum lose its flavour on the bedpost overnight?

(Answers at foot of page)

PHILOSOPHICAL STATEMENTS OF THE DAY

'Enjoy money while you have it. Shrouds don't have pockets.'

'Pornography is in the groin of the beholder.'

Brain-teaser Answers

1) Comedy shows, because laughing is good for the system. (Medical fact, honest!) 2) Only on days without a 'Y' in them. 3) Arthur Daley and Terry McCann. 4) Nicholas Parsons. 5) Thirty per cent, or an Austrian gerbil; whichever is the larger.

January 8th

This week's (reasonably) lucky star forecast is for

♍ ♈ **ARIES** ♎ ♏

An exciting time ahead, when you become the first person to break wind in Bucharest without ironing the wallaby. Just remember: never put off 'til tomorrow what you can put off 'til the day *after* tomorrow.

Happy Birthday to Shirley 'titanic-tonsils' Bassey (1937) and David Bowie (1947) – the only superstar who speaks fluent Gibberish.

(NB – only 351 days 'til my birthday, so get thinking about my present while there's still time! I'll leave the final choice to you, but I'd quite like a 21-gun soufflé, or a self-basting poodle.)

January 9th

Happy Birthday to Richard 'expletive deleted' Nixon (1913).

THE KENNY EVERETT GUIDE TO SURVIVAL IN THE TWENTIETH CENTURY

(and how to get rid of boring people)

Bored out of your tree by some-one? Here are some sample lines guaranteed to get rid of brain-numbingly dreary ding-bats:

1) 'I can't remember the last time you opened your mouth. All I know is that you haven't closed it since.'
2) 'I've got a surefire way of making certain everyone has a great time at your next party – invite them all over to your place . . . and then go out to a movie.'
3) 'Hi, frog-breath . . .'
4) 'That dress fits you like a glove – shame it doesn't fit you like a dress . . .'

January 10th

Happy Birthday to the man blondes have more fun with, Rod Stewart (1945).

Uncle Ken's Agony Column

I recently received this very disturbing letter which I would now like to share with you.

Dear Uncle Ken...

For security reasons I am unable to reveal my name. Suffice to say that I am Prime Minister of a small country called Britain. For some time now I have been conducting a long-distance romance with what I can only describe as the President of a large continent.

He is tall, dark and wrinkled as a prune. But I love him with all my heart, my kidneys, liver and onions. I've told him that I'll follow him to the ends of the earth, and he's said that he'll probably be able to arrange it. I want to know if unrequited love and adoration is bad for the lumbar region.

Yours Aloofly,

P.M. (Anon)

Uncle Ken writes:

Dear PM. (Anon),

You are suffering from a very common complaint known as sycophancyobsequiousitis. The best known remedy is to smother yourself with cream cheese and lie in a darkened room for 48 hours while sticking pins into a life-size effigy of Jemima Puddle-duck. Please do not hesitate to contact me again if you have any more trouble with the man in the anorak.

January 11th

PHILOSOPHICAL STATEMENT OF THE DAY

'Schizophrenia beats dining alone.'

I once saw a great piece of graffiti in New York which said: 'So I'm cured of schizophrenia – but where am I now that I need me . . . ?'

While you're figuring that one out, consider the words of Billy Connolly:

> Roses are red
> Violets are blue
> I'm a schizophrenic
> And so am I

January 12th

Bathroom Brain-teasers

1 How do you spell fridge?
2 What is blennophobia?
3 What is the capital of Helmut Schmidt?
4 How much food does the average person eat in a lifetime?
5 When did you last brush your teeth?

(Answers at foot of page)

Brain-teaser Answers

1) Sometimes. 2) Fear of slime (honest!). 3) Not if I see you first. 4) 50 tons (true). 5) Mind your own business.

Many Happy Returns of the day to Michael Aspel (1933) and Des O'Connor (1864). Aspel once told me that he and Des always exchanged birthday presents: 'Because I like him, I ask for a copy of his latest record, and because he likes me he doesn't send one.'

Are you a dismal failure with members of the opposite sex? Does your idea of a dirty weekend involve changing the oil filter on the car? At no extra expense, here is a selection of CHAT-UP LINES GUARANTEED TO WORK/FAIL DISMALLY (delete as applicable):

1) 'I think the great body of mankind would agree that yours is the great body of mankind.'
2) 'You have a beautiful bone structure: it holds you together, and it tears me apart.'
3) 'You're so gorgeous, I bet even the bags under your eyes are made by Gucci.'

January 13th

DEPARTMENT OF THINGS YOU NEVER NEEDED TO KNOW BUT WHICH MIGHT COME IN HANDY WHEN YOU'RE STUCK FOR SOMETHING TO SAY . . .

Today being the thirteenth day of the month, millions of triskaidekophobics all around the world will be huddled under their duvets, keeping well out of harm's way.

Triskaidekophobia is the morbid fear of the number 13 and – when a Friday the Thirteenth comes around – America loses a billion dollars through absenteeism, cancellations and loss of business. Famous triskaidekophobes include Napoleon, J. Paul Getty, Herbert Hoover and Franklin Roosevelt who refused to sit at a dinner table of thirteen people; rather than tempt fate, he would insist that his secretary make up the numbers to fourteen.

Triskies always seek to prove their point by citing the ill-fated Apollo 13 space mission which was launched at 13.13 Central Standard Time from pad 39 (the multiple of 13) and had to be aborted on April 13th. All of which goes to prove something, but I'm not entirely sure what.

January 14th

Happy Birthday to actors and extremely good eggs Peter Barkworth (1929) and Richard Briers (1934).

THOUGHT FOR THE DAY

The brain is a wonderful organ. It starts working the moment you get up in the morning, and doesn't stop until you get into the office.

THE
KENNY EVERETT
GUIDE TO SURVIVAL IN THE
TWENTIETH CENTURY

(and how to win friends and influence aubergines)

Part Six:
Never poison a Peer of the Realm without first getting his permission in triplicate.

January 15th

A right royal **Happy Birthday** to Princess Michael of Kent (1945).

This week's Superstar horoscope is for

↗ ♐ **GEMINI** ♓ ♊

A good time for property matters, but a bad time for dressing as a goat and smearing yourself with Marmite.

The best time to do that is when the Moon moves into Saturn, or when there's nothing worth watching on telly. Above all, remember that eighty per cent of married men commit adultery in America – the rest commit adultery in Europe.

January 16th

Let's open a bottle and celebrate Prohibition, which began on this day in 1920.

(Wanna know how 'bootleggers' got their name? Well, I'm going to tell you anyway: it dates back to Ye Olde Days of Ye Wilde West when the Yanks flogged naughty booze to the Indians – apparently the Booze Boys used to conceal bottles of hooch in their boots.)

W.C. Fields was known for being fond of a drop or two. He said, 'A woman drove me to drink, and I never even had the courtesy to thank her.'

As for wrinkly old sweetheart, George Burns, he's a moderate boozer: 'It only takes one drink to get me loaded. Trouble is, I can't remember if it's the thirteenth or the fourteenth . . .'

January 17th

Happy Birthday to Muhammed Ali (1942), King of the Crimpers Vidal Sassoon (1928) and Al Capone (1899–1947).

Not many people know this, but Al Capone's successor as chief baddie was Mafia boss Don Fettucine. Well-known for his ruthless attitude towards people, he was once walking on a beach near his home when he heard the sound of frantic cries for help coming from the sea.

'Help . . . help!' yelled the drowning man. 'Help! I can't swim . . . ! I can't swim . . . !'

Don Fettucine narrowed his eyes and said, 'So what? I can't play the piano, but I don't go round making a fuss about it.'

THOUGHT FOR THE DAY

The opposite of talking isn't listening. The opposite of talking is waiting.

January 18th

Happy Birthday to barmy botanist David Bellamy (1933) and to Cary Grant (1904–1987) who's no doubt being suave and sophisticated on a cloud somewhere.

Uncle Ken's Agony Column

Dear Uncle Ken...

I am writing this letter slowly because I know you can't read very. My problem is this: I have great trouble finishing my sentences which, as you can imagine, gets very. Sometimes I get as far as the last word and then I just. Can you suggest anything which will help me overcome this awful?

Yours Sincerely,

Algernon P. Buttock

Uncle Ken writes:

Dear Mrs Buttock,

In cases such as yours there is only one remedy. Unfortunately I can't for the life of me remember what it is.

Thank you for taking the trouble to write. (My invoice will follow shortly.)

January 19th

Happy Birthday to legendary Swedish barman, Lars Tordersplease (1891), Michael Crawford (1942) and Dolly Parton (1946).

(N.B. — THIS IS NOT A SEXIST BOOK! I PLEDGE MY HONOUR AND MY TROTH THAT THERE WILL BE NO DOLLY PARTON BOOB JOKES IN THIS HIGH-CLASS TOME. (Oh, well, maybe just one . . . ?))

According to an apocryphal (it's OK, look it up later) tale, our Dolly was once auditioning for *Romeo and Juliet*. The casting director wasn't too sure about her talents as an actress, but was heard to say, 'Who cares if she can act – she can sure as hell lean over a balcony!'

THOUGHT FOR THE DAY:

'Marriage is like a bank account: you put it in, you take it out, you lose interest.'

January 20th

Happy Birthday to Edwin 'Buzz' Aldrin (1930) – the second man to land on the moon. To give you an idea of how fast Buzz and the boys travelled, they left earth with two rabbits and when they got to the moon, they still had only two!

And hundreds of **Happy Birthdays** to George Burns (1896). He says that he's now getting to the age when just putting his cigar in its holder is a thrill.

Burns was once asked about his philosphy on acting and he replied, 'Acting is all about honesty. If you can fake that, you've got it made.'

January 21st

Astro-loogical personality profile for all those born under the sign of

~~ AQUARIUS ☉

(January 21st - February 19th). A charming bunch of people, Aquarians are renowned for making good diplomats, skilled doctors and excellent *chilli-con-carne*. Generally speaking they are loyal friends, excellent lovers and reliable work-mates. The fact that they find it hard to whistle in tune should not be held against them.

Happy Birthday to Placido 'Titanic Tonsils' Domingo (1941), Benny Hill (1925) and Telly Savalas (1924).

January 22nd

Queen Victoria died on this day in 1901.

According to a friend of mine, Victoria's descendant Prince Charles is preparing to record his own version of Frank Sinatra's 'My Way'. He's going to call it, 'One Did It One's Way'.

This week's spifferoony star-forecast is for

♎ ♋ LIBRA ♌ ♍

Not a good time for planning major career moves. Nor is it a good time for planning to invade Czechoslovakia. It will only end in tears and sick, and there won't be enough sausage-rolls to go round.

Your lucky vegetable is Sylvester Stallone.

January 23rd

Bathroom Brain-teasers

1 What is studied by an oologist?
2 What is studied by an omelettist?
3 How many nerks are there in a grummet?
4 What is the definition of the Jewish dilemma?
5 Why are black clothes warmer than white clothes?

(Answers at foot of page)

Brain-teaser Answers

1) Birds' eggs (True!). 2) Omelettes. 3) Not as many as you'd like to think. 4) Free ham. 5) Because black surfaces absorb heat; white surfaces reflect heat (True!).

January 24th

Happy Birthday to Neil 'Forever in Blue Jeans' Diamond (1941) and Bamber 'Forever Doing University Challenge' Gascoigne (1935).

As Woody Allen would be the first to agree, it's never too early to think about death. I therefore take great pride in presenting the following SUGGESTIONS FOR YOUR TOMBSTONE:

'Here lies (XXXX). Born (XXXX), Died (XXXX) . . . but never got the hang of it.'

Here's one for a vengeful wife:

> Here lies my husband
> I hope he squirms
> While being devoured
> By a bunch of worms.

And one I saw in a village churchyard:

> I hope I fare well
> But I've just a suspicion
> Death won't pay me
> As it did my mortician.

January 25th

THE
KENNY EVERETT
GUIDE TO SURVIVAL IN THE
TWENTIETH CENTURY

(and how to avoid attracting the attention of the vice squad):

> Part 26 (b):
> Never insert a suppository
> with a fork.

And while we're on the subject of animals (yes, I know, but I want to put in this daft quote by Robert Benchley and I can't find any other way of doing it) just remember: 'a boy can learn a lot from a dog: obedience, loyalty, and the importance of turning around three times before lying down . . .'

January 26th

Happy Birthday to former Goon Michael Bentine (1922) and actor-turned-salad-dressing manufacturer Paul Newman (1925).

Today's also the anniversary of the day when I said goodbye to my lovely Mercedes motor-car. The circumstances were rather tragic, and it was all the fault of a deaf-as-a-post odd-job man called Bill. He turned up out of the blue one day and asked if I wanted any jobs done. 'Sure,' I said, 'you can paint the porch green.'

Three hours later he came back and told me he'd finished. He pocketed ten quid and climbed onto his bike . . . As he pedalled off into the sunset, he called over his shoulder, 'Pleasure doing business with you, Mr Everard. By the way, that's a Mercedes, not a Porsche.'

Aaargh . . . !

January 27th

Happy Birthday to William Randolph Hearst (1908). Hearst was the model for the classic movie *Citizen Kane*, directed by the late great Orson Welles who once said, 'I hate television. I hate it as much as peanuts. But I can't stop eating peanuts.'

Happy Birthday also to a true genius, Wolfgang Amadeus Mozart (1756–1791). The clever little fellow heard his first symphony at the age of four and transcribed the whole score from memory. At five years old he began composing his first symphony, and went on to write over six hundred of the fabbest toons in the history of fab toons.

January 28th

Happy Birthday to M.A.S.H. star Alan Alda (1936) and Mikhail Baryshnikov (1948).

DAFT DEFINITIONS:

An accountant: someone who can put two and two together and make a living.

An intellectual: someone who can listen to the William Tell Overture without thinking of The Lone Ranger.

Australian foreplay: 'Are you awake?'

A fad: something that goes in one era and out the other.

Imagination: the thing that keeps a woman company when her husband is out late at night.

January 29th

Happy Birthday to Tony Blackburn (1943), Germaine Greer (1939) and actor, drinker and child-lover W.C. Fields (1880–1946). He was also a bit of a philosopher on the quiet, remembered for many *bons mots* including, 'It's a funny old world – a man's lucky if he can get out of it alive.' And, 'Few things in life are more embarrassing than having to inform an old friend that you have just got engaged to his fiancée.'

This week's happy horoscope is for

SAGITTARIUS

A murky deed will shortly come to light. This should teach you to take a closer interest in matters of personal hygiene. Your lucky colour is penguin.

January 30th

Bathroom Brain-teasers

Who popularised the following catchphrases?

1 Hello, my darlings?
2 Wakey-wakey?
3 Nice to see you, to see you nice!
4 All done in the best possible taste.
5 Can you please help me finish my spinach? I seem to have lost my grandmother and am very concerned about her kippers. Please can you fix my Magi-mix before my husband gets home?

(Answers at foot of next page)

Happy Birthday to Vanessa Redgrave (1937).

January 31st

Happy Birthday to Phil Collins (1951). On this day in 1606 Guy Fawkes was hanged, drawn and quartered, which made him very sore indeed and put paid to his plans for a quiet night at home watching telly.

Actress and *bonne viveuse* Tallulah Bankhead was born in 1903. She went on to make classic movies and live a turbulent life, once describing herself as 'pure as the driven slush'. But she had few regrets: 'The only thing I regret about my life is the length of it. If I had to live my life again, I'd make the same mistakes, only sooner.'

The best Tallulah tale of all is when she was greeted by an old admirer who said, 'Tallulah, darling, I haven't seen you for over forty years!' Tallulah peered at him and said: 'I thought I told you to wait in the car.'

What a woman!

February 1st

Clark Gable – the mucho-macho man who makes Arnold Schwarz-
enegger look like Bonnie Langford – was born on this day in 1901.
TRUE STORY: Gable once bared his torso in a film called *It
Happened One Night*. So powerful was the impact of his bulging
mega-hairiness that men all over America stopped wearing vests,
and several vest manufacturers actually went out of business!

Happy Birthday also to humorist S.J. Perelman (1904–1979).
Perelman wrote many of the scripts for the Marx Brothers
movies, and penned such unforgettable lines as:
GROUCHO: ' . . . you've got the brain of a four-year-old boy, and I
bet he was glad to get rid of it.'

February 2nd

Happy Birthday to Farrah
Fawcett (1946), Elaine Stritch
(1925), Hughie Green (1920)
and lovely Les Dawson (1933) –
famed for his deep and abiding
affection for his mother-in-law:
'The mother-in-law thinks I'm
effeminate: not that I mind because beside her, I am!'

THE
KENNY EVERETT
GUIDE TO SURVIVAL IN THE
TWENTIETH CENTURY

(and how to avoid being sent to
the Tower of London)

Part 35 (d):
Never eat baked beans just before an audience with the Queen

Brain-teasers Answers

1) Charlie Drake. 2) Billy Cotton. 3) Bruce Forsyth. 4) The
Lovely Me. 5) Oddly enough, this catchphrase has yet to catch on.
If you are a struggling young comedian and would like to adopt this
phrase as your own, please send a cheque for £5,000 to the following
address:
KENNY EVERETT'S PERSONALISED CATCHPHRASE SER-
VICE, PO BOX 244, The Bahamas.

February 3rd

Bathroom Brain-teasers

1 What is the capital of Australia?
2 What is the difference between a tree and Joan of Arc?
3 How long will a dose of cyanide take to kill you?
4 The total weight of Heinz baked beans sold in Britain each year is equivalent to that of how many African elephants?
5 Why Do Fools Fall In Love?

(Answers at foot of next page)

February 4th

Uncle Ken's Agony Column

Dear Uncle Ken...

I have recently developed a terrible fixation. It's ruining my life and I'm turning to you as a last resort. I've fallen hopelessly in love with myself. Quite simply, I think I'm the most amusing, sexy, gorgeous, intelligent person I've ever met. The problem is that this passion is unrequited. I never return my phone calls, I don't write letters to myself, and when I pass myself in the street I just cross to the other side and ignore me. Have you ever come across a case like mine?

Bewildered Millionaire pop-star

Uncle Ken writes:

Dear George Michael,

Yes, I have come across a case like yours. It was blue, with a leather strap, and I stubbed my toe on it near Victoria Station.

February 5th

Looking ahead to this week's lucky stars, the pick of the bunch is for

♏ **SCORPIO** ↗

As the world's only possessor of felt-tipped elbows, you must now resist the temptation to french-polish your poodle more than once a week. Prepare for a shock on Tuesday when the ghost of Queen Victoria calls to give you her favourite recipe for steak-and-kidney pudding.

Happy Birthday to Fwank Muir (1920) and the divine Charlotte Rampling (1946).

February 6th

Many Happy Returns of the day to Zsa-Zsa Gabor (1919) – although she won't thank me for revealing her age). Zsa-Zsa is chiefly known for a) her many marriages, and b) her many marriages. Asked how many husbands she's had, she replied, 'You mean, apart from my own . . . ?'

And Bob Hope once cracked, 'Zsa-Zsa Gabor got married as a one-off, and it was so successful she turned it into a series.'

Happy Birthday also to Denis Norden (1922), who is one of the world's great sweetie-pies and who invented the much-copied 'It'll Be Alright On The Night' blooper show. He's also responsible for some of my Favourite Funnies like:

'Full-frontal nudity has now become accepted by every branch of the theatrical profession, with the possible exception of lady accordion-players.'

Many Happy Returns to everybody's favourite comedian, Ronald Reagan (1911).

Brain-teaser Answers

1) Canberra (no, not Sydney). 2) One is made of wood, the other is Maid of Orleans. 3) 15 minutes. 4) 20,000. 5) Fill in your own answer to this one.

February 7th

Happy Birthday to Charles Dickens (1812–1870), among whose many accomplishments was the fathering of ten children (!)

Going to a club or a bar tonight? Try these CHEEKY CHAT-UP LINES:
'I don't believe we've met. I'm Mr Right.'
Or: 'I'm afraid I don't dance very well. But I'd love to hold you while you do.'

February 8th

Happy Birthday to Jack Lemmon (1925) and James Dean (1931–1955).

PHILOSOPHICAL STATEMENT OF THE DAY
'Whoever said money can't buy happiness didn't know where to shop.'

And if you're on your uppers at the moment, here are a few facts to make you green with envy:

At the last count, the Sultan of Brunei was worth 14.7 *billion* pounds! Other mega-rich folk who are down to their last few billion include American hardware tycoon Sam Walton (£5.1 billion); American chocolate-bar king Forrest Mars (£3.3 billion) and our own dear Queen (£4.4 billion).

February 9th

Mrs Patrick Campbell (George Bernard Shaw's verbal sparring partner) was born on this day in 1865. It was dear old Mrs P.C. who once said of sex: 'It doesn't matter what you do in the bedroom as long as you don't do it in the street and frighten the horses.'

It's a barmy old world, and to prove it, here's a genuine news flash which caught my eye a while ago:

'Eyewitness Mr John Charles said, "The party given by the British Deaf Association was going very well. Then one group of the deaf began to attack the other and the next thing you knew thousands of them were at it. When the police arrived they tried to restore order with a loud-hailer. But this was no use, as they were insulting each other in sign language."'

February 10th

Happy Birthday to Larry Adler (1914) and Joyce Grenfell (1910–1979), who once defined happiness as 'the moment when you get out of your corsets at night'. Having spent many hours dressed up as Cupid Stunt, I know just what she means!

FASCINATING FACTS DEPARTMENT: Having briefly toyed with the notion of becoming a priest, I spent many hours studying the Bible. I'll bet you didn't know that the word 'girl' occurs only once in the Bible, but there are eighteen dogs, no cats, and 46,227 uses of the word 'and'.

February 11th

Happy Birthday to one of the greatest inventors of all time: Thomas Edison (1847–1931). He was the geezer who said that 'genius is one per cent inspiration and ninety-nine per cent perspiration' – which must have made him rather unpleasant to sit next to on the tube. As every schoolboy knows, Edison discovered electricity. Apparently he was spring-cleaning the house one day, and he found it down the side of the sofa. Some people are just born lucky, I guess.

February 12th

Happy Birthday to Charles Darwin, who's best remembered for his theory 'Origin of the Species'. He's less well-remembered for his other works like 'Origin of the Chinese Takeaway' and 'Origin of the Jet-propelled Chicken', but, given the choice, I expect he'd rather be remembered for his theory that we're all descended from apes.

Astro-loogical time again, and look out

♑ ♒ VIRGO ♍ ♈

– it's your turn this week: Plenty of opportunities to impress your friends are just around the corner – especially when it is announced that you are to receive the Nobel Prize for gerbil-juggling. Your lucky Norwegian King was Haakon Haakonarson. (But as he died in 1263, there's not much point in relying on him to bale you out any more.)

February 13th

THE
KENNY EVERETT
GUIDE TO SURVIVAL IN THE
TWENTIETH CENTURY

(and how to avoid hospitalisation)

Part 1:
Never play leapfrog with a Unicorn.

Happy Birthday to Oliver Reed (1938).

William and Mary came to the throne in 1689. (Later that same year they moved to the kitchen, and then ventured as far as the Wendy House. But they were eventually forced to return to the throne following an encounter with a particularly spicy prawn vindaloo.)

February 14th

The most smoochy-woochy day of the year, and what better time to consider the antithesis of romance?

Larry Brown once confessed that 'the most romantic thing a woman ever said to me was "are you sure you're not a cop?"'

Mae West believed that 'love conquers all things, except poverty and toothache.'

But by far the most unromantic thing in the world was the following definition of love according to the delegates at the first International Conference on Love and Attraction: Love is 'the cognitive-affective state characterised by the intrusive and obsessive fantasising concerning reciprocity of amorant feeling by the object of the amorance . . .' (Huh . . . ?)

February 15th

More proof (as if it were needed) that it's a Mad Mad Mad world comes from this recent American newspaper report:

'Told that the bones of Private Eddie Slovik, the only American soldier to be shot for desertion since the Civil War, had been misdelivered from France to San Francisco instead of to Detroit, Mr Jackson Henry of Interstate Airways said: "these things happen all the time."'

February 16th

Many Happy Returns of the day to John McEnroe (1959).

The Fab Four's first mega-hit 'Please Please Me' reached No. 1 on this day in 1963, and the world was never the same again.

Uncle Ken's Agony Column

Dear Uncle Ken...

Mine is a very embarrassing problem. I'm addicted to blanc-mange. Ordinarily, this would not cause too many difficulties, but my particular problem is the fact that I like *wearing* it. Every morning, I coat myself in at least three different flavours (natur-ally taking great care to ensure that the colours match). The real trouble comes when I leave the house because – as you can imagine – the whole lot has dropped off by the time I get to the office. Can you suggest anything to help?

Sticky of Salford

Uncle Ken writes:

Dear Sticky,

This is nothing to be ashamed of. Some of our best-known public figures enjoy dressing up in all kinds of food. Rudolph Nureyev is known to wear a thin coating of Bovril when he goes to the opera, and Jeremy Irons is seldom seen in public without a topcoat made entirely from red cabbage.

February 17th

Bathroom Brain-teasers

The following are all real words. What do they mean?
1 Brachiate.
2 Crapula.
3 Horripilating.
4 Machicolated.
5 Nictitation.

(Answers at foot of next page)

Happy Birthday to Barry Humphries (1934), best friend and manager of Housewife Mega-star Dame Edna Everage, Sir Les Patterson and many other magnificent entertainers.

February 18th

Happy Birthday to Yoko Ono Lennon (1934), Ned Sherrin (1931) and John Travolta (1954).

Today's Loo Laff

I was on a bus some years ago when an enormously fat woman staggered on board and was dismayed to find there was nowhere for her to sit. She puffed and panted, and hung on to a strap for some time, all the while glaring around at the rest of the passengers, most of whom were men.

'Isn't anyone going to offer me a seat?'

A very thin man stood up and said quietly: 'Well, I'm prepared to make a small contribution . . .'

February 19th

This week's lucky sign of the zodiac is

♉ ♊ **TAURUS** ♌ ♎

An especially good time for all foreign Heads of State born under this sign. For all others born under this sign, things will go from bad to worse, so become a foreign Head of State now, while there's still time.

Brain-teaser Answers

1) To swing from limb to limb – like Tarzan. 2) Hangover. 3) Getting goose-bumps. 4) Gap-toothed. 5) Winking. (Imagine using 'nictitating' in a real sentence: 'Your place or mine,' he nictitated . . .)

February 20th

Astro-loogical personality profile for all those born under the sign of

♓ ♋ **PISCES** ♏ ♐

(February 20th – March 20th): Much of the Piscean's energies will be expended searching for peace, harmony and something to get that nasty stain out of the carpet. In a recent poll, eight out of ten Pisceans left only two; of these two, one went off to become a missionary in Africa, and the other one didn't.

Happy Birthday to Jimmy Greaves (1940) and Sidney Poitier (1927).

PHILOSOPHICAL STATEMENT OF THE DAY

'If it weren't for the last minute, nothing would ever get done.'

February 21st

Happy Birthday to Jilly Cooper (1937), or 'Jolly Sooper' as she is known. Full of good advice, she once advised people 'never drink black coffee at lunch – it will only keep you awake in the afternoon.' She also has a fairly jaundiced view of men: 'the male is a domestic animal which, if treated with firmness and kindness, can be trained to do most things.'

THE KENNY EVERETT GUIDE TO SURVIVAL IN THE TWENTIETH CENTURY

(and how to avoid getting nasty messes all over the floor)

Never attempt to open a sardine tin with your nipples.

February 22nd

Happy Birthday to Bruce Forsyth (1928), Edward Kennedy (1932) and goody-two-shoes George Washington (1732–1799). Washington's family doesn't sound very cosy; apparently he had to address his mother as 'Honourable Madam'.

Ever played the anagram game, when you take a famous name and jumble it around? Try these for size . . .
Tory big-wig Nigel Lawson = We All Sign On
British Labour leader Neil Kinnock = I knock Lenin
Former Soviet Big Cheese Konstantin Chernenko = Another Ten N. Kinnocks.
Former Argentinian Big Cheese General Galtieri = El large Argie nit.

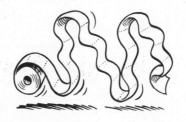

February 23rd

Happy Birthday to diarist Samuel Pepys (1633–1703). A bit of a fruit-cake by all accounts, Pepys celebrated his thirty-sixth birthday by toddling along to Westminster Abbey and kissing the embalmed body of Catherine de Valois, who had once been married to Henry V. Each to their own, I suppose, but personally I'd prefer a night out with the Dagenham Girl Pipe-Cleaners.

PHILOSOPHICAL STATEMENT OF THE DAY

'The best thing about a cocktail party is the invitation.'

February 24th

Many Happy Returns of the day to Dennis Waterman (1948).

PERSONALITY POSERS: Exercise your grey matter (or your pink matter for that matter, it really doesn't matter . . .):

1) Your best friend's other half tells you that he/she is seeing someone else – would you tell your best friend, or would you rather be a fish?
2) If I offered you £10,000 to eat a live worm, would you do it?
3) If you could look into the future and find out what will happen to you in ten years' time, would you want to know?

(Please seal your answers in an envelope and feed them to the cat.)

February 25th

Happy Birthday to George Harrison (1943) who, with typical understatement, once said, 'If you have to be born, and if you have to be in a rock band, it might as well be The Beatles.'

Let's celebrate with a burst of BEATLES' BRAIN-TEASERS:
1 Whom did Ringo Starr replace as drummer with the Fab Four?
2 In which song does 'Father McKenzie darn his socks'?
3 In which year was the famous John and Yoko 'bed-in' campaign?
4 How much were The Beatles paid for their first lunchtime gig at the Cavern in Liverpool?
5 What was the original title of 'Yesterday'?

ANSWERS: 1. Pete Best.   2. Eleanor Rigby.   3. 1969.
4. £5!   5. 'Scrambled Eggs'.

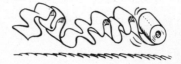

February 26th

Be brave, my little dumplings, because it's time for a touch of the old prognostications as we gaze forwardwards into the future with a little help from the Utterly Infallible Fate-Forecasting Service:

A good time ahead for all

GANGERIANS

except for the fact that many will be arrested for making improper suggestions to an under-age chicken tikka. Just remember the profound words of the twelfth-century psychic, Wayne P. Huckleberry The Thirteenth: 'He who buys Val Doonican records better have a damn good reason.'

February 27th

Happy Birthday to Elizabeth Taylor (1932). The much-married Miss Taylor might appreciate one or two of these gems:

'Every woman should marry – and no man.' (Benjamin Disraeli)
'When a man brings his wife flowers for no reason – there's a reason.' (Molly McGee)
'Marriage is popular because it combines the maximum of temptation with the maximum of opportunity.' (George Bernard Shaw)
'Marriage is marginally better than slicing your fingers off on the edges of a rusty tin of Whiskas.' (Anon)

February 28th

Happy Birthday to golf commentator Peter Allis (1931). Personally, I've never had the slightest desire to join the show-biz golfing Mafia; it seems a rather daft way to spend your time. The late, great Jack Benny once said: 'Give me my golf clubs, fresh air and a beautiful partner, and you can keep my golf clubs and the fresh air.'

February 29th

Happy Birthday to the man who had the longest name in the world: Adolph Blaine Charles David Earl Frederick Gerald Hubert Irvin John Kenneth Lloyd Martin Nero Oliver Paul Quincey Randolph Sherman Thomas Uncas Victor William Xerxes Yancy Zeus . . . one name for each of the twenty-six letters of the alphabet! And his surname was (deep breath) Wolfeschlegelsteinhausenbergerdorft!!

Can you imagine filling in a tax return if you had a name like that? By the time you'd completed the form, you'd be on to a new tax year.

Incidentally, I liked the suggestion for a new, simplified tax-return form:

'How Much Money Did You Make Last Year? Mail It In.'

March 1st

Uncle Ken's Agony Column

Dear Uncle Ken . . .

I am writing to you with a problem which concerns my family. I am married with two children, and my husband has recently begun an affair with my step-sister's first cousin's half-brother's cleaning lady. To make matters worse, I have just fallen in love with my mother's step-son's Auntie Flo's plumber's pen-pal from Zimbabwe. And on top of all that, I have tremendous difficulty in getting my Yorkshire puddings to rise properly.

Any advice would be much appreciated.

Uncle Ken writes:

Pardon?

PHILOSOPHICAL STATEMENT OF THE DAY
'Happiness is good health and a bad memory.' (Ingrid Bergman)

March 2nd

Happy Birthday to Concorde, which took off for the first time on this day in 1969. Although I'm not frightened of flying, the whole business bores me rigid. As Mel Brooks once said: 'If God had meant us to fly, he'd have given us tickets.'

March 3rd

Many Happy Returns of the day to Alexander Graham Bell (1847–1922). As you probably know, he invented the telephone. But you may not be aware of the fact that old Alex never got on very well with his mum. In fact, his dying words are believed to have been, 'Gone! And never called me mother!'

(Think about it . . .)

THE
KENNY EVERETT
GUIDE TO SURVIVAL IN THE
TWENTIETH CENTURY

(and how to observe the country code and not get locked up a lot)

When visiting the country, never attempt to milk the village bobby.

March 4th

Please fasten your cigarettes and extinguish your seat-belts because here comes today's **Astro-loogical Forecast** for

♍ ♈ **ARIES** ♎ ♏

There can be little doubt you are now entering one of the most important periods of your life. When you get there, take the second turning on the left, go past the traffic lights, and remove all articles of clothing. In times of family crisis, just remember: when a man steals your wife, there is no better revenge than letting him keep her.

Happy Birthday to the composer of some of the world's fabbest twiddly-bits, Antonio Vivaldi (1678–1741).

March 5th

Bathroom Brain-teasers

1 What are the five letters of the alphabet used most often in the English language?
2 In 1867, America paid £1,450,000 for what?
3 What name is given to a man who has more than one wife?
4 Why is it so difficult to get the wrappers off those little triangles of cheese?
5 How many brain cells does an average person lose per day from the age of thirty?

(Answers at bottom of page)

Russian Big Cheese (and extremely uncuddly person) Joseph Stalin went to join the Great Collective in the Sky on this day in 1953. In spite of everything, Russians seem to have maintained their sense of humour if Soviet comedian Yakov Smirnoff is anything to go by. He said:

'In the United States you have freedom of speech. You can go up to Ronald Reagan and say, "I don't like Ronald Reagan." In the Soviet Union you have the same thing. You can go up to Gorbachev and say, "I don't like Ronald Reagan."'

Brain-teaser Answers
1) E,T,O,A, and N. 2) Alaska. 3) Bigamist/Masochist. 4) No, I don't know either, but isn't it aggravating? 5) 100,000!

March 6th

Happy Birthday to Frankie Howerd (1922) and also to the first woman in space, Valentina Tereshkova (1937).

Today's Loo Laff

A newly-married woman was less than thrilled with her husband's performance between the sheets, so she asked him what she could do to liven things up a bit.

'Well,' he told her, 'what I'd really like is for you to moan a bit while we're making love. That would really make a big difference.'

The couple retired to the bedroom and things began to go well. The wife whispered, 'Is this the right moment? Shall I start to moan now?' Her husband nodded.

'Right,' she said, 'how come you never help with the flamin' washing-up . . . ?'

March 7th

THE BATTLE OF THE SEXES:
Since the dawn of time (and probably long before then as well) men and women have been having a go at each other. Here's a selection of some of the best insults:

'A man without a woman is like a neck without a pain.' (Anon)
'Women need men like fish need bicycles.' (Another non)
'A woman's place is in the wrong.' (James Thurber)
'Women rule the world . . . no man has ever done anything that a woman either hasn't allowed him to do, or encouraged him to do.' (Bob Dylan)
'Women have their faults
Men have only two:
Everything they say,
And everything they do.' (Yet another non)

March 8th

Happy Birthday to Channel Four Supremo Michael Grade (1943). Grade – a former boss of mine when he was Head-of-Everything-That-Is at the British Broadcorping Castration – once told his Channel Four predecessor Jeremy Isaacs: 'If at first you don't succeed, you're fired.'

And while we're talking about the Amazing Grades, Lew Grade has come up with some good 'uns in his time. When Franco Zeffirelli was over budget on a Lew Grade production of the film *Jesus of Nazareth*, he explained to Grade that part of the reason the costs were so high was because there had to be twelve apostles. Grade reportedly looked at his balance sheet, lit another cigar and said: 'Twelve! So who needs *twelve*? Couldn't we make do with six?'

March 9th

Happy Birthday to Amerigo Vespucci who followed in Colombus's footsteps and gave his name to America (1454–1512). Just as well he didn't give his surname to the country; somehow the United States of Vespuccia doesn't have the same ring to it . . .

THE KENNY EVERETT GUIDE TO SURVIVAL IN THE TWENTIETH CENTURY

When planning a bank robbery, never use a pogo-stick as your getaway vehicle.

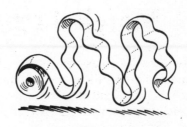

March 10th

Many Happy Returns to Prince Edward (1964).

Uncle Ken's Agony Column

Dear Uncle Ken...

I am writing to you about my husband, who has taken to being very rude to me of late. Admittedly he's been under a lot of strain recently with the new job, especially as he now has 6,000 men under him (he works in our local cemetery). But it all came to a head because I went to the doctor on Monday and my husband went with me. The doctor put a small tube in my mouth and told me not to talk for ten minutes. My husband offered to buy it from him. When I told him that I wanted a coat made from real animal skin, he went out and bought me a donkey jacket. Can you suggest anything to remedy the situation?

Yours, Disillusioned of Dimpleford
(P.S. I was going to send you five pounds for your advice, but I'd already sealed the envelope.)

Uncle Ken writes:

Dear Disillusioned,

In my experience there is only one way to deal with people like your husband: have him marble-ised.

March 11th

Happy Birthday to media mega-tycoon Rupert Murdoch (1931) and also to former Prime Minister and champion pipe-smoker, Harold Wilson (1916). (A friend of mine is a heavy smoker. She read in *Time* magazine that smoking is bad for you, so she decided to give up reading *Time* magazine.)

Feeling nervous about what the week holds for you? Feeling unsure of yourself? Feeling frightened of the fickle finger of fate? Well, so you should be – especially if you're

CAPRICORN

Friends may be urging you to make concrete proposals, or iron girders, depending on which way the wind's blowing. Remember the words of the poet Algonquin: 'he who hesitates is . . . er, he who hesitates is . . . um . . . er . . .'

March 12th

Happy Birthday to singing superstar Liza Minnelli (1946) and one of the great comedians of all time, Max Wall (1908).

REVENGE
Apropos of nothing in particular, I liked the story of the woman who was told by her lover that their affair was at an end, and that she had to be out of the house by Monday. To avoid an ugly scene, he went away for the weekend. On his return, he noticed the phone was off the hook and picked up the receiver to hear the sound of the Speaking Clock . . . all the way from Sydney, Australia! His angry girlfriend had taken her revenge by leaving the line hooked up for over 48 hours!

March 13th

Happy Birthday to Joe Bugner (1950) and Tessie O'Shea (1918).

Today's Loo Laff

When God was trying to sort out the Ten Commandments, Moses climbed up to the top of the mountain to engage in a bit of round-the-table negotiation. After some hefty bargaining sessions, he reported back to the throng.

'Right, you lot,' he said. 'We've sorted the whole thing out, and there's good news and bad news. The good news is that we've got it down to Ten.'

The crowd cheered loudly. A small voice cried out, 'And what's the bad news, Moses?'

'Well,' he said, 'the bad news is that adultery is in.'

March 14th

Many Happy Returns to Michael Caine (1933) whose real name is Maurice Micklewhite – and Not Many People Know That! **Happy Birthday** also to comedian Jasper Carrott (1945); his real name was Jasper Cauliflower, but he changed it because he thought it sounded silly.

And while we're celebrating, let's wish a **Happy Birthday** to Albert Einstein (1879–1955). He once tried to simplify his Theory of Relativity by explaining: 'When a man sits with a pretty girl for an hour, it seems like a minute. But let him sit on a hot stove for a minute – and it's longer than an hour. That's relativity.' (Personally I'm still none the wiser.)

March 15th

THE
KENNY EVERETT
GUIDE TO SURVIVAL IN 44BC

(and how to avoid being stabbed several times by people you think are on your side)

Today sees The Ides of March, the day on which Julius Caesar died in 44 BC.

Never trust a man who organises a plot to end your life.

FASCINATING FACTS (Number 001):
Did you know that American comedian Sid Caesar is in no way related to the Roman emperors of the same name?

March 16th

Happy Birthday to American comedian Jerry Lewis (1926). In 1963 he signed a five-year television contract worth twelve and a half million pounds! (The show was cancelled thirteen weeks later.)

Today's Loo Laff

A maid was having a row with her aristocratic mistress, Lady Muck-Snooty.

'I've had enough of working for you,' she said. 'And what's more, you're not as great as you think you are. In fact, your husband told me that I'm a better cook than you, I'm better at house-keeping, and I'm much more beautiful as well!'

Getting no reaction from Lady Muck-Snooty, the maid continued, 'And I'm much better in bed than you are!'

Lady Muck-Snooty peered down her nose at the girl.

'I suppose my husband told you that as well?'

'No,' grinned the maid. 'The gardener did.'

March 17th

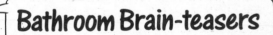

Bathroom Brain-teasers

1 What does a 'musophobe' fear?
2 What are the four small bones at the base of the spine called?
3 In order to remain alive, what part of its body can a cockroach most afford to do without?
4 What used to be the most common form of execution in Mongolia?
5 Until 1859 it was an offence in England not to celebrate Guy Fawkes Day – true or false?

(Answers at foot of next page)

March 18th

Once again we gaze up at the astrologicals and ask, 'What does fate have in store for us this week?' And the answer if you're a

is this:
You will be pleasantly surprised this week when Lew Grade offers to *Raise The Titanic* again and erect it underneath your duvet. This will result in your bedroom being placed under close arrest and grilled for seven minutes, turning regularly. Serve with a sprinkling of Parmesan cheese.

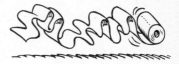

March 19th

Like to win a million pounds, a safari holiday for two, and a night out with the sex-symbol of your choice . . . ? Well, wouldn't we all?

In the meantime, console yourself by seeing how smart you are with this BIGGEST TALLEST LONGEST HIGHEST QUIZ:

1. What is the world's largest desert?
2. What is the world's biggest ocean?
3. Which pop star has the world's longest nose?
4. What is the world's longest river?
5. What is the world's worst joke?

ANSWERS: 1) Sahara. 2) Pacific. 3) Barry Manilow.
4) Nile. 5) How do you stop a cold going to your chest? Tie a knot in your neck.

Brain-teaser Answers

1) Mice. 2) The coccyx (or, in my case, Albert, Miranda, Charles and Wendell). 3) Even if you cut off a cockroach's head it can still live for several weeks! 4) Nailing the offender in a coffin and leaving him to die. (Remind me not to book a summer hol in Mongolia). 5) True.

March 20th

Among the unrecognised heroes of our age are the graffiti artists who work tirelessly, day and night, in order to bring a little amusement into our dreary lives.

The Official Graffiti Top Five is as follows:

1. If voting changed anything, they'd make it illegal.
2. Death is life's way of telling you to slow down.
3. God is not dead. He is alive and working on a much less ambitious project.
4. Is a *pas de deux* a father of twins?
5. Q. How do girls get minks?
   A. The same way minks get minks.

March 21st

Astro-loogocal personality profile for

♍ ♈ **ARIES** ♎ ♏

(March 21–April 20):
Deeply superficial in all respects, Arians love to mix with other people – as long as they're rich or beautiful, or both. Let it never be said that Aries-born people are gullible idiots. Other things which should never be said include: *a*) Bum; *b*) Not if I see you first; *c*) Your breath smells like mouldy cheese.

Aries' lucky stone is Mick Jagger, and their lucky colour is most unsuitable for the complexion.

March 22nd

Happy Birthday to Andrew LloydWebber, otherwise known as Andrew LloydsBank (1948).

Uncle Ken's Agony Column

Dear Uncle Ken...

My marriage has been going through a sticky patch recently. In fact, I haven't kissed my wife for nearly forty years. The reason for this is that she won't let me kiss her when I'm drunk and when I'm sober I don't want to. Things have gone from bad to worse and the other day I came home from work earlier than expected and caught my wife in bed with my best friend.

What words of wisdom do you have on this matter?

Cheesed-Off of Chingford

Uncle Ken writes:

Dear Cheesed-Off,

Stay late at the office.

March 23rd

Happy Birthday to four-minute miler Sir Roger Bannister (1929) and comedian Jimmy 'Whacko' Edwards (1920).

CUDDLY KEN'S POETRY CORNER:

Mary had a little lamb
It had a touch of colic
She fed it brandy twice a day
And now it's alcoholic.

PHILOSOPHICAL STATEMENT OF THE DAY

'Life is what happens to you while you're busy making other plans.' (John Lennon)

March 24th

Happy Birthday to Malcolm Muggeridge (1903) and Tommy Trinder (1909).

Today's Loo Laff

En route to Scotland from London, a man was trying to doze off in the top bunk of a sleeping compartment. He was woken by the sound of someone tapping from the bunk below.

'Are you awake?' asked a husky female voice.

'Yes. Is something the matter?'

'It's terribly cold down here. I wonder if you'd mind letting me have an extra blanket?'

The man thought for a moment. 'I've got a much better idea,' he said. 'Why don't we pretend we're married?'

The woman giggled. 'That's a great idea.'

'Fine,' said the man. 'Now get your own bloody blanket!'

March 25th

Oodles of **Happy Birthdays** and squillions of happy returns to pop mega-super-hyperstar and champion-party-giver Elton John (1947). (There, that should get me an invitation to his next bash.) Elton once went through a bad patch and tried to 'end it all', but fortunately he lived to tell the tale. He told me shortly afterwards, 'It was a very Woody Allen-type suicide attempt: I turned on all the gas, and left the windows open.'

Star time again, loo-lovers, and today it's the turn of

♐ ♑ GEMINI ♓ ♊

Seldom has your career been better aspected, and seldom has your hair been so appallingly greasy. Business matters will go from bad to worse, and then move quickly on to Torquay where they'll star in a summer season with Des O'Connor. In times of stress remember the words of Evan Davies: 'Nice guys finish last, but we get to sleep in.'

March 26th

Happy Birthday to Leonard Nimoy, otherwise known as Mr Spock (1931) and to Supremely talented Diana Ross (1944).

And now we cross live to our TRUTH IS STRANGER THAN FICTION correspondent:

Many years ago in Sweden a man decided to make a few kröne by selling his body for medical research. Not long afterwards, he came into a lot of money and asked to buy back the rights to his body. Doctors refused to allow him to do this, went to court and won a possession order. Furthermore, they won considerable damages from the man because he had had two teeth extracted without their permission!

March 27th

PHILOSOPHICAL STATEMENT OF THE DAY

'Nouvelle cuisine is food that is so beautifully arranged on the plate, you know someone's fingers have been all over it.' (Julia Child)

THE
KENNY EVERETT
GUIDE TO SURVIVAL IN THE
TWENTIETH CENTURY

(and how to avoid getting very flattened by large lorries)

(Part 84):
Never have a picnic in the fast lane of a busy motorway.

WORLD'S GREATEST BOOK TITLE: *How to Raise Your I.Q. by Eating Gifted Children* (Lewis B. Frunkes).

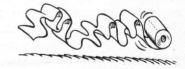

March 28th

Bathroom Brain-teasers

1 Why is Nicholas Parsons in *The Guinness Book Of Records*?
2 Why is Nicholas Parsons?
3 What is peculiar about the way a camel moves?
4 How many quires make up a ream?
5 What is a newspaper editor?

(Answers at foot of page)

Happy Birthday to former British Prime Minister James Callaghan (1912).

March 29th

Happy Birthday to Dirk Bogarde (1921), Neil Kinnock (1942) and Michael Parkinson (1935).

Uncle Ken's Agony Column

Dear Uncle Ken...

I am engaged to be married to a man who is my fiancé. It's a curious arrangement, but we've grown used to it. So far I've

---

Brain-teaser Answers

1) He is joint holder of the record for the longest-ever after-dinner speech: 11 hours! 2) Someone has to be. 3) It simultaneously lifts both feet on one side. 4) Twenty. 5) Someone who separates the wheat from the chaff . . . and then prints the chaff!

managed to preserve my honour, but the other day I asked him if he believes in sex before marriage. He replied, 'not if it holds up the ceremony'. I then asked him why elephants are grey, and he replied, 'so you can tell they're not blackberries'. My question is this: what do you call a nine-foot gorilla?

Yours Sincerely,

Old Chestnut of Cheshunt.

Uncle Ken writes:

Dear Old Chestnut,

The answer to your last question is 'Sir'. (Please do not waste my time with more questions along these lines. I have serious work to do and, moreover, my masseuse is due at any minute.)

March 30th

Happy Birthday to former Python star Eric Idle (1943) and also to Radio Caroline, Britain's first pirate radio ship which started up in 1964, and paved the way for Yours Truly to become a disc-jockey on Caroline's rival, Radio London. (I once nearly got fired from Radio London for saying the word 'orgasm' on the air. I'd heard Ed Stewart use it in conversation, but I didn't know what it meant, so I went on the air and said that listening to the Beatles' new disc-ipoo made me want to orgasm. When the Big Cheeses discovered I'd used the word in all innocence, they decided to keep me on, but only on the condition that I never again used a word on the wireless unless I was sure of its meaning.)

March 31st

Many Happy Returns to actor and 'super-stud' Warren Beatty (did you know he is Shirley MacLaine's half-brother?). I can't remember who, but someone once said that if there really turns out to be such a thing as reincarnation, he'd like to come back as Warren Beatty's finger-tips!

PHILOSOPHICAL STATEMENT OF THE DAY

Nobody ever forgets where he buried the hatchet.

April 1st

In spite of the fact that today is April Fool's Day, no one's going to pull the wool over your socks, are they? Especially if you're born under the sign of LIBRA and are wise enough to arm yourself with this week's **Astro-loogical Forecast:**

♎ ♋ **LIBRA** ♌ ♍

You are perfect in every way . . . except for the additional pair of knees which are cur-rently beginning to sprout from your nostrils. If people start to stare, the best solution is to explain that they came direct from the manufacturer and are still under guarantee.

April 2nd

Happy Birthday to Sir Alec Guinness (1914), posher-than-the-Queen actress Penelope Keith (1939) and king of the canoodlers, Casanova (1725). For reasons which must be left to the imagination, Casanova never had any problems with women (in fact, according to legend he was only given the brush-off once). American Max Kauffmann could have learned a thing or two from Casanova, if this description of his attempts at flirtation is anything to go by: 'She was a lovely girl. Our courtship was fast and furious – I was fast and she was furious.'

April 3rd

Happy Birthday to Tony Benn (1925), Doris Day (1924) and Marlon Brando (also 1924). Brando once dismissed the whole of his fellow professionals in the following way. 'An actor's a guy who, if you ain't talking about him, ain't listening.'

THE
KENNY EVERETT
GUIDE TO SURVIVAL IN THE
TWENTIETH CENTURY

(and how to win friends and influence people)

Never poke out the eyes of anyone you really want to lend you money.

April 4th

Uncle Ken's Agony Column

Dear Uncle Ken...

I'm very depressed at the moment because, after fifteen years of labouring under a misapprehension, I've recently discovered that I'm not world-famous sex-symbol Joan Collins. I am, in fact, Reg Spong, a heavy-goods vehicle driver, and I'm married with three children and an aspidistra called Wendy. You can imagine what a shock this has been to me, and to my entire family who – up until now – have never had any cause to doubt my word. My wife is threatening to divorce me and she's almost certainly going to demand custody of my entire collection of lip-gloss and shoulder-pads. What can I do to rectify the situation?

Yours Sincerely,

Joan/Reg

Uncle Ken writes:

Dear Joan/Reg,

In situations like this, my advice is always to take your mind off things by becoming immensely wealthy. You'll be surprised how quickly all your worries disappear.

April 5th

Happy Birthday to the legendary Bette Davis (1908). She celebrated her seventieth birthday by having a 'black' party. She wore black, the guests wore black, there were wreaths not flowers and even the food was black!

PERSONALITY POSERS:
Test your moral fibre with this Character Conundrum:

You want to watch *Neighbours*, but your spouse is keen to watch a documentary about Black Forest gâteaux-makers of the twelfth century. Do you *a*) give in gracefully, or *b*) stove in your spouse's head with the nearest length of lead-piping?

April 6th

By extraordinary coincidence, today sees the birthday of both Paul Daniels (1938) and Harry Houdini (1874–1926). Houdini's real name was Ehrich Weiss, and when he was a bijou escapologist-ette he passed many happy hours learning how to contort his body. After a lot of practice he learned to pick up pins with his eyelashes and thread needles with his toes!

PHILOSOPHICAL STATEMENT OF THE DAY

'If love is the answer, would you mind repeating the question . . . ?'

April 7th

Hello, good evening and **Happy Birthday** to David Frost (1939), who has been known to come up with a clever put-down or two like: 'He has left his body to science, and science is contesting the will . . .'

Bathroom Brain-teasers

1 What was peculiar about the death of King Philip the Handsome of Spain?
2 On a daily basis, what is the average amount of water used by the average European adult?
3 Nelson's body was returned to England in a barrel of rum – true or false?
4 In how many *Carry On* movies has Margaret Thatcher starred?
5 What is a 'diophthalm'?

(Answers at foot of page)

April 8th

This week's toe-curling, hair-gripping, pencil-sharpening Star Forecast is for all those born under the sign of

♋ **CANCER** ♉ ♌

A trying time ahead, and also a week when you will feel the urge to use the word 'endomorphic' in every sentence. In times of self-doubt, just remember that it's never too late to wiggle the grummet, but it takes a smart man to flangle the grint.

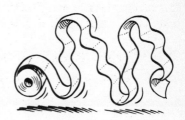

Brain-teaser Answers

1) His wife kept his body in her bed for three years after he died!
2) 40 gallons. 3) True! 4) Don't be so silly. 5) Something with two eyes.

April 9th

Happy Birthday to American humorist Tom Lehrer (1928), who obviously considered himself to be an under-achiever. He once remarked mournfully: 'It is sobering to consider that when Mozart was my age he had already been dead for a year . . .'

Today's Loo Laff

A little girl arrived very late for school and apologised to the teacher. 'I'm sorry I'm late, sir, but my Dad was in a bad mood and I had to come by myself.'

Sir frowned and said, 'Never mind, but I hope you've done your homework properly. Remember yesterday, I told you to study the geography of India and Pakistan?'

'Yes, sir.'

'Good, then can you tell me where the Pakistan border is?'

'Yes, sir, in bed with my Mum. That's why Dad was in such a bad mood.'

April 10th

Happy Birthday to smoothie actor, bridge-player and former professional footballer Omar Sharif (1932).

Browsing through the bookshelves of my dear friend Dawn Chorus the other day, I came across some fascinating-sounding volumes, like:

Great Buildings of the Twentieth Century by R.K. Tecture.
How to be Brilliant at Maths by Lois Carmen Denominator.
My First Biology Book by M. Brio.
The Politician by Eliza Lott.
The Big Question by Jemima R. Sking.
The Beginning of America by Bertha Venation.
The Jewish Guide to Beautiful Hands by Manny Q. Rist.

April 11th

PHILOSOPHICAL STATEMENT OF THE DAY

'Everything in life is ten minutes too long.' (Simon Booker)

Ever wanted to be in show business? To become a star and be in the papers all the time? Well, in my experience, the best thing about having a famous face is that you sometimes get a good table in restaurants. One of the worst things is that you are often on the receiving end of THE POISON PEN OF THE CRITICS:

'She (Sarah Brightman) looked like one of the chorus girls in "The Muppets". Her voice will do wonders for the sale of earplugs.'

On Julie Andrews: 'So sweet she could give you tooth decay at fifty paces.'

Jack Tinker on Pamela Stephenson: 'While she may look as fresh as a dairymaid, she also sings like a dairymaid who has stood in something even fresher.'

April 12th

Happy Birthday to David Cassidy (1950) and the Earl of Limerick – Under Secretary of State for Trade from 1972 to 1974 (b. 1930) And to celebrate his ermine-ness's birthday, here's a limerick I have composed with my own bare hands:

> There was a Secretary of State
> Who was late for a date at a fête.
> When asked where he'd been
> Replied, 'with The Queen.'
> But everyone thought he was just name-dropping.

(OK, smarty-pants, *you* have a go . . .)

April 13th

Uncle Ken's Agony Column

Dear Uncle Ken...

For some years now I have been trying to wean myself off a terrible addiction to porridge. At first I thought I could handle it. I started in a small way with the occasional bowl at breakfast-time, but pretty soon I moved on to forty or fifty bowls a day. I've recently taken to snorting it through a straw. It's wrecking my career, my family and my waistline. What shall I do?

Uncle Ken writes:

This is no time for beating about the bush, or counting your chickens before they spoil the broth. My advice is to spend a week or two recuperating in Ian Botham's truss.

April 14th

On this day in 1865 Abraham Lincoln was assassinated. Uncannily, he had said on the morning of that fateful day: 'Do you know, I believe there are men who want to take my life. And I have no doubt they will do it.' After his death, eighty letters containing death-threats were discovered in his desk drawer.

THE

KENNY EVERETT

GUIDE TO SURVIVAL IN THE

NINETEENTH CENTURY

(and how to get the most out of a trip to the theatre):

If you're President of America, never ignore eighty death threats.

April 15th

Time to look ahead to what the fates have in store for us this week, and today's perfectly proportioned, palpably preposterous prognostication is for

♑ ♒ **VIRGO** ♍ ♈

A week in which to be wary of small green men offering get-rich-quick schemes. Also a week to be wary of people who ask if they can pull out your eyeballs. Just remember: when the going gets tough, the tough go shopping.

Happy Birthday to Jeffrey Archer (1940) and Leonardo da Vinci (1452–1519). The *Titanic* sank on this day in 1912.

April 16th

Three special birthdays to celebrate today. **Many Happy Returns** to well-known typing error Spike Milligna (1918) – famous for extreme goonery, and for having played a major part in the downfall of Adolf Hitler. Of his time in the army, he says: 'The army works like this: if a man dies when you hang him, keep hanging him until he gets used to it.'

Happy Birthday also to Peter Ustinov, who summed up the complicated business of love in a film called *Romanoff and Juliet*: 'I can see from your utter misery, from your eagerness to misunderstand each other, and from your thoroughly bad temper, that this is the real thing.'

And **Happy Birthday** to Charles Chaplin (1889–1977), probably sitting on a cloud somewhere and having a good laugh at all of us. In his time, comedy was a great deal more straightforward than it is nowadays. He said, 'All I need to make a comedy is a park, a policeman and a pretty girl.'

April 17th

Bathroom Brain-teasers

1 On which part of the body would you wear puttees?
2 On which part of the body would you wear nuttees?
3 What do Dennis Waterman and Honoré de Balzac have in common?
4 What do Magnus Magnusson and Samantha Fox have in common?
5 What was Bing Crosby's real first name?

(Answers at foot of page)

PHILOSOPHICAL STATEMENT OF THE DAY

'A fanatic is someone who can't change his mind and won't change the subject.' (Winston Churchill)

Brain-teaser Answers

1) Legs. 2) Nuts. 3) They both married Polish countesses. 4) Absolutely nothing. 5) Harry.

April 18th

RIDICULOUS RIDDLES

1 All that we managed to find we threw away; everything we couldn't find we kept – what are they?

2 What has a cat's whiskers, a cat's head, a cat's tail, and isn't a cat?

3 What has a hundred legs, but cannot walk?

4 Take three away from this six-letter word and you'll be left with one – what is the word?

5 Which side of a sparrow has the most feathers?

RIDDLE ANSWERS:

1) Head-lice. (Charming, eh?).   2) A kitten.   3) Fifty pairs of trousers.   4) Throne.   5) The outside.

THE KENNY EVERETT GUIDE TO SURVIVAL IN THE TWENTIETH CENTURY

(and how to avoid starting the day off on the wrong foot)
Part 43:
Never make muesli in a blender using your own nuts.

April 19th

Happy Birthday to sex-thimble Dudley Moore (1935).

And yes – it's official. Today's the day when the first 'doctor' joke was unleashed on the world. To celebrate, here are a couple from the medical chestnut chest:

'Doctor, doctor, can you give me something to stop my hands shaking?'

'Dear me, do you drink a lot?'

'No doctor, I spill most of it.'

'Doctor, doctor, is there anything you can do to help me? I keep seeing pink stripey crocodiles.'

'Really? How disturbing. Have you seen a psychiatrist?'

'No, just pink stripey crocodiles.'

April 20th

Adolf Hitler was born on this day in 1889. Many books have been written about this odious little creep, but it is not commonly known that he suffered from a morbid fear of flatulence! (This may explain a great deal.)

Personally, I can't begin to understand why Hitler had such a thing about the Jews. How could anyone not adore a race who come up with such great jokes? Like this one:

Manny was run over by a truck and a priest was summoned from a nearby church to help him through his last minutes on earth.

'Manny,' whispered the priest, 'do you believe in the Father, the Son and the Holy Ghost?'

Manny's eyes flickered open. 'Typical! I'm lying here dying, and he asks me riddles!'

April 21st

Happy Birthday to Her Majesty-ness the Queen (1926), and also to Rumpole's creator, John Mortimer (1923), who was also a brilliant practitioner of the law: 'No brilliance is needed in the law. Nothing but common sense, and relatively clean fingernails.'

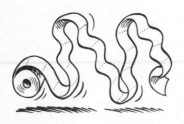

Astro-loogical personality profile for all those born under the sign of

♉♊ **TAURUS** ♌♎

(April 21st – May 21st): Taureans admire talent in others, value peace and quiet in their own lives and have a soft spot for Cornish pasties. (One Taurean of my acquaintance recently left his wife for a Cornish pastie and – as a direct result – lost the ability to tie his own shoelaces.)

April 22nd

What better way to begin this page than by looking ahead to the signs of the Zodiac . . .? (Actually, there are probably many better ways, but it's time for this week's Star Forecast.) And, what do you know, it's for wise words of St Trevor of Alopecia: 'He who casts the first aubergine will never get perfect reception on BBC2.'

♈ ♓ ♌ **LEO** ♉ ♊ ♋

There now seems to be little point in denying your involvement with the squirrel. In these uncertain times, you would do well to remember the

---

April 23rd

Happy Birthday to Shirley Temple-Black (1928).

Uncle Ken's Agony Column

Dear Uncle Ken...

I'm having a very hard time making my boyfriend do exactly what I want. The basic problem is one of communication. Last night he asked me to go out with him but I said I couldn't because I was going to see *Romeo and Juliet*. He told me to bring them too.

My question is this: if two's company, and three's a crowd, what are four and five . . . ?
Yours Sincerely,

Uncle Ken writes:
Nine.

April 24th

Happy Birthday to Clement Freud (1924), Shirley MacLaine (1934), Barbra Streisand (1942).

EVERETT'S ETIQUETTE:
How many times have you been stumped at a dinner or a party and simply not known what to do: which knife to use, which glass to drink from, or how to engage in polite conversation?

Debrett's Etiquette and Modern Manners is a fascinating book which will help you through any awkward situation, and suggests the following opening gambits as a sure-fire way of keeping the conversation flowing:

'What a cold December we are having. If you weren't in England, where would you like to be at this time of year?'

'If you were the Queen, which opera/ballet/play would you choose to have performed for your Gala?'

Talk about Dullsville. I ask you, CAN YOU IMAGINE . . .?!?!

Try these guaranteed ice-breakers instead:

'What a hideous nose! Would you like the name of a good plastic surgeon?'

'Excuse me, I think I'm going to be extremely ill all over your Boeuf Stroganoff.'

'Seldom have I met anyone as excruciatingly dull as you are. I hope you are plagued by piles for the rest of your life.'

April 25th

Happy Birthday to the patron saint of disc-jockeys Guglielmo Marconi who – bless his cathodes – invented radio (1874–1937).

PHILOSOPHICAL STATEMENT OF THE DAY

'Some are born great, some achieve greatness, and some hire public relations officers.' (Daniel Boorstin)

Graffiti Corner

Beethoven was so deaf he thought he was a painter.
A bachelor is an unaltared male.
How come there's only one Monopolies Commission?

April 26th

Happy Birthday to American comedienne Carol Burnett (1936) and writer Anita Loos (1893–1981), who penned the brilliant *Gentlemen Prefer Blondes* which contained the immortal line 'She always believed in the old adage – leave them while you're looking good.'

Today was the day when William Shakespeare was baptised in 1564. Among the many controversies which have raged over the greatest writer the English language has ever known (apart from Claire Rayner), is whether or not he actually wrote all the plays with which he's credited. Walter Raleigh and Queen Elizabeth I are sometimes thought to have been responsible for some of The Master's works, but nothing has ever been proved.

Old Bill shuffled off this mortal coil in 1616, and he wrote his own tombstone-farewell to the world:

> Good friend, for Jesus sake forbear
> To dig the dust enclosed here.
> Blest be the man yt pares these stones,
> And curst be he yt moves my bones.

(You'd have thought he'd be able to spell properly, wouldn't you?)

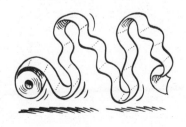

April 27th

Happy Birthday to Samuel Morse 1791–1794. His last recorded words were: ·· −− −−

Today's Loo Laff

A famous pop star consulted a Harley Street surgeon about a rather embarrassing problem.

'Everything's fine, doctor, except that every time I sing I break wind. The curious thing is that there's no odour, just a horrid noise, and it's getting very embarrassing.'

The doctor asked for a demonstration, so the pop star launched into his latest hit. Sure enough, there was the sound of a loud raspberry.

'You see what I mean, doctor?' said the shamefaced mega-star. 'There's no pong, but it's highly embarrassing.'

The doctor said: 'I can give you some tablets for the wind, but I'm afraid you'll have to have an operation on your nose.'

'On my *nose*? What on earth for?'

'Because, young man, it stinks like hell!'

April 28th

Happy Birthday to American entertainer and highly explosive sex-bomb Ann-Margaret (1941). She once said: 'I was thinking of leaving my body to medical science. The only trouble is, all the doctors want it now.'

Happy Birthday also to the menacingly masterful Jack Nicholson (1937).

THE KENNY EVERETT GUIDE TO SURVIVAL IN THE TWENTIETH CENTURY

Never clean out the bath with your tonsils. Always borrow someone else's.

April 29th

Happy Birthday to Emperor Hirohito, of Japan, the world's longest-reigning monarch, born 1901.

Ah, April 29th. One of my favourite dates! In fact, I have several favourite dates, like 3rd January, 16th October, 22nd July, and I've cunningly concealed them in the pages of this book. See if you can spot them, but don't do it now, cause it's time for this week's Star Forecast:

♍ ♈ **ARIES** ♎ ♏

Beware of people who speak with forked tongue. Also, beware of people who speak with forked fingers. But, above all, beware of people who insist on showing you their holiday snaps of Torquay. Your lucky word beginning with 'M' is *BUDGERIGAR*.

April 30th

BEAUTY CORNER
(No, not a list of helpful hints about eye-shadow, and how to keep young by smearing gulls' eggs all over your skin, but a selection of sayings about one of my favourite topics.)

'The human soul needs actual beauty more than bread.' (D. H. Lawrence)

'The best thing is to look natural, but it takes make-up to look natural.' (Calvin Klein).

'A handsome man is not quite poor.' (Spanish proverb)

'All heiresses are beautiful.' (Dryden)

'I'm tired of all this business about beauty being only skin-deep. That's deep enough. What do you want – an adorable pancreas?'

'When I go to a beauty parlour, I always use the emergency entrance. Sometimes I just go for an estimate.' (Phyllis Diller).

May 1st

Many Happy Returns of the day to the divine Joanna Lumley (1946), who introduced me to the world's most infuriating tongue-twister. Forget about 'she sells sea-shells'... Peter Pepper, eat you heart out... just try saying:

PEGGY BABCOCK

out loud ten times in quick succession.

See? It's impossible, right? Now try:

RED LORRY
YELLOW LORRY

THE
KENNY EVERETT
GUIDE TO SURVIVAL IN THE
TWENTIETH CENTURY

Part 96:
Never pre-heat a hand-grenade in your microwave oven.

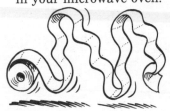

May 2nd

Happy Birthday to Engelbert Humperdinck (1936) and Bing Crosby (1904–1977) who's probably on a cloud somewhere, crooning away merrily.

Today's Loo Laff

This story concerns the time when Frank Sinatra was in a restaurant, and was approached by a nervous young man.

'Excuse me, Mr Sinatra, my name is Melvyn and I was wondering if you'd do me a big favour.'

'What kind of favour, sonny?' growled Ol' Blue-Eyes.

'Well, I'm on a first date with a girl and I'm keen to make a good impression. I'd be really thrilled if you could stop by at our table on your way out and just say, "Hi Melvyn, good to see you again."'

Sinatra was in a good mood that night, so he agreed. Later that evening he passed by the young couple's table and said: 'Hi Melvyn, good to see you again.'

Melvyn looked up and snapped, 'Don't bother me now, Frankie. Can't you see I'm busy?'

May 3rd

Bathroom Brain-teasers

1 Which of James Bond's girl-friends hit Russell Harty on TV?
2 On average, how many hairs are there on each inch of your scalp?
3 When under threat, how does a possum try to avoid capture?
4 What species of animal was Tarka the Otter?
5 What is the most savage creature known to mankind?

(Answers at foot of page)

Many Happy Returns of the day to 'enry Cooper (1934).

Brain-teaser Answers

1) Grace Jones. 2) 1,200 (But not if your name is Bruce Forsyth). 3) By pretending to be dead. 4) Don't be so silly. 5) A tax inspector.

May 4th

Happy Birthday to Audrey Hepburn (1929) and Eric Sykes (1923).

DAT'S ALL FOLKS . . . ! (A selection of famous last words)

Florenz Ziegfeld, American Showman:
'Curtain! Fast Music! Lights! Ready for the last finale! Great! The show looks good, the show looks good!'

Arthur Spong, hunter:
'What herd of rhinocer . . . ?'

W.C. Fields, comedian:
'On the whole, I'd rather be in Philadelphia.'

Dylan Thomas, Welsh poet:
'I've had eighteen straight whiskies. I think that's the record . . .'

May 5th

Happy Birthday to Monty Python star and extremely sweet-natured chappie Michael Palin (1943). **Happy Birthday** also to Karl Marx (1818–1883) . . . (was he the one with the cigar . . . ?)

Uncle Ken's Agony Column

Dear Uncle Ken . . .

Having recently recovered from a charisma-bypass operation, I now find myself plagued by a new problem which is threatening to ruin my life. It is simply the fact that I cannot complete a sentence without including the first part of the original sentence in the conversation, and it is quite simply the most aggravating having recently recovered from a charisma-bypass operation, I now . . . there I go again.

Can you imagine how infuriating it must be to having recently recovered from a charisma-bypass operation . . . oh, really, this is ridiculous; forget the whole thing, and I'm very sorry to have troubled you, having recently recovered . . . (AAARGGH!!!).

Yours having recently recovered from a charisma-bypass operation. . . .

May 6th

Are you sitting comfortably? Good, then I'll begin with this week's **Astro-loogical Forecast**, and this time it's for

♉ ♊ **TAURUS** ♌ ♎

You're unlikely to be able to do anything to impress members of the opposite sex this weekend. You're also unlikely to be asked to head a United Nations enquiry into bladder control. In fact, there are so many things you won't be asked to do this week that I can't possibly list them all here. You may as well face facts and give the garden gnome an extra coat of Stilton.

Happy Birthday to Orson Welles (1915–1987) and Sigmund Freud (1856–1939). Famed for his research and theories into sexual symbolism, Freud seemed to recognise that not all so-called phallic symbols have sexual connotations. He is reputed to have once said: 'Sometimes a cigar is just a cigar.'

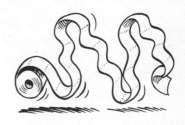

May 7th

Happy Birthday to one of the greatest composers of all time, Peter Ilyich Tchaikovsky (1840–1893).

On this day in 1945, the world breathed a huge sigh of relief as the Germans surrendered unconditionally.

Happy Birthday (sort of) to Eva Peron (1919–1952) who made a bit of a name for herself in Argentina, and earned the eternal gratitude of Elaine Paige.

May 8th

Happy Birthday to wildlife wizzo Sir David Attenborough (1926).

Today's Loo Laff

A sexologist was delivering a lecture on the fact that the happiest people are those who make love most often. To prove his point, he asked those members of his audience who made love every day to raise their hands. A handful of people did so, all beaming broadly. He then asked for a show of hands from all those who made love once a week. About half the audience raised their hands – none of them looking ecstatic.

Then he asked for an indication of how many people made love once a month. The remainder of the people sheepishly put their hands in the air.

Sitting at the back of the lecture hall was an old man, his face positively glowing with pleasure and happiness.

'I notice you didn't raise your hand, sir,' said the sexologist. 'May I ask how often you make love.'

'Certainly,' beamed the old man. 'Once a year.'

'Well, you look remarkably happy, considering; may I ask why you're so cheerful?'

The old man's smile grew even wider. 'Certainly. It's tonight! It's tonight!'

May 9th

Happy Birthday to 'piano-man' Billy Joel (1949), and playwright Alan Bennett (1934). I admire people who have a wonderful way with words, and few have wonderfuller ways than what he does.

'Life, you know, is rather like opening a tin of sardines. We're all of us looking for the key.'

Asked to describe Greek-born writer Arianna Stassinopoulos,

he said she was '. . . so boring, you fall asleep halfway through her name.'

And he also wrote of his work: '. . . What I'm above all primarily concerned with is the substance of life, the pith of reality. If I had to sum up my work, I suppose that's it really: I'm taking the pith out of reality . . .'

May 10th

Bathroom Brain-teasers

1 What does a pyrophobe fear?
2 What does a clampophobe fear?
3 What is the collective noun for a group of larks?
4 What is the collective noun for a group of traffic wardens?
5 What would you use a sphygmomanometer to measure?

(Answers at foot of page)

Happy Birthday to the long-suffering Denis Thatcher (1915) and the wonderfully witty actress Maureen Lipman (1946), who is blessed with a Yiddisher Momma to end all Yiddisher Mommas.

When Maureen published a book of magazine pieces entitled *How Was It For You?* her mother phoned and asked, 'How was *what* for you . . . ?'

Brain-teaser Answers

1) Fire.   2) Being clamped.   3) An exaltation.   4) A peril.   5) Blood pressure.

May 11th

Many Happy Returns of the day to the composer of 'White Christmas', Irving Berlin (1888). And **Happy Birthday** to sur-real-supremo Salvador Dali who was born in 1904.

Surreal joke

Q: How many surrealists does it take to change a light-bulb?
A: The fish. (. . . huh . . ?)

And **Happy Birthday** also to American satirist Mort Sahl (1927), who delights in taking the mickey out of things, viz: 'Beverly Hills is very exclusive. For instance, their fire depart-ment won't make house-calls . . .'

May 12th

Happy Birthday to the Lady of the Lamp, Florence Nightingale (1820–1910), and also to the king of the limerick writers, Edward Lear (1812–1888), who almost certainly didn't write this one:

There once was a much-beloved Queen
Who one day misplaced her spleen.
She found it and mused,
   'We Are Not Amused.
For Heaven's sake, where have you been?'

May 13th

Happy Birthday to general genius Stevie Wonder (1950).

Q: To whom did Stevie Wonder dedicate his fab hit 'Happy Birthday'?
A: Martin Luther-King.

Working under laboratory conditions, a team of doctors has produced conclusive evidence that smoking is one of this country's leading sources of statistics.

All of which has nothing to do with the fact that today's the day when we look ahead to the day after today, and then the day after that. Yes, folks, it's Star Time!

⚆ ♑ GEMINI ♓ ♊

A tough time for anyone wanting to increase the size of their overdraft, and an even tougher time for anyone wanting to invent a cure for the common cold which can also be used as an eyebrow pencil. In times of despair, always remember Googie Withers . . . but at her time of life, can you blame her?

May 14th

Many Happy Returns of the day to the man who invented heat and cold: Gabriel Fahrenheit (1686–1736).

Uncle Ken's Agony Column

Dear Uncle Ken...

Please can you advise me about a problem I have? I recently returned from Hong Kong, where I had a suit made for me. On my return to England, I noticed there was a hump in the back of the jacket, and on inspection it transpired that the tailor was still at work. Will I be arrested for aiding and abetting an illegal immigrant?

Uncle Ken writes:

Not unless your name contains more than three letters of the alphabet. If this is the case, then I should ask for mitigating circumstances to be taken into consideration, or a nice cup of tea – whichever is the shorter.

Glad to have been of help.

May 15th

WARNING, this section is catching . . .

Since the dawn of time (and probably before then as well) people have been coming up with catchy phrases, either to sell a product or to ram home a message. See how many you recognise:

'All human life is there.' Which newspaper?

'Any time, any place, anywhere.' Which drink?

' . . . refreshes the parts other beers cannot reach.' Which lager?

'Nothing over sixpence.' Old slogan for which chain of stores?

'Don't leave home without . . .' What?

'The weekend starts here.' Which 1960s TV pop show?

ANSWERS *News of the World;* Martini; Heineken; Woolworth; American Express; 'Ready Steady Go!'

May 16th

On this day in 1929, the first Hollywood Oscar ceremony took place. (One of my favourite acceptance speeches was made by the legendary Jack Benny. He said: 'I don't deserve this, but then, I have arthritis and I don't deserve that either. . . .')

Today's Loo Laff

A teenage couple – Billy and Jane – were getting on very well. After a few dates Jane invited Billy to spend an evening at her house. 'My parents will be out at a concert,' she told Billy with a broad smile and a wink, 'so we can have a good time . . . if you know what I mean.'

On the afternoon of the Great Day, a very nervous Billy stopped off at the chemist's to buy some condoms. He was relieved to find that the chemist was a very helpful man who was full of advice about what to do when the big moment came.

That night he arrived at Jane's house. The door was opened by her mother. 'Come on in, Billy,' she said. 'My husband's just getting ready, and then we'll be off.'

At that moment, Jane's father appeared at the door, with Jane standing at his side.

'G-g-g-good evening,' stammered Billy. 'Er . . . Jane, I think I'd like to go to the concert with your Mum and Dad.'

Jane frowned. 'Really? I didn't know you liked classical music?'

'I don't,' hissed Billy. 'But then, I didn't know your father was a chemist!'

May 17th

Bathroom Brain-teasers

1 How do male moths pursue female moths when it's dark?
2 How do male hedgehogs make love to female hedgehogs?
3 What is the derivation of the word 'posh'?
4 Can you spell MARZIPAN?
5 What would you be if you were hypermetropic?

(Answers at foot of page)

KIDDIES' CORNER:
'Keep smiling – it makes the grown-ups wonder what you're up to.'

Brain-teaser Answers

1) By sense of smell. 2) Very carefully. 3) An abbreviation used by wealthy travellers booking passage on ships to the East: 'Port Out, Starboard Home' – i.e. on the cooler side of the ship. 4) No. 5) Long-sighted.

May 18th

Today was the birthday of film director Frank Capra (1897), who made one of my all-time favourite movies, *It's A Wonderful Life*, starring Jimmy Stewart. **Happy Birthday** also to politician Norman St John Stevas (1929) who, when a member of Mrs Thatcher's Cabinet, is credited with giving her the nickname 'Attila The Hen'.

And **Happy Birthday** to philosopher Bertrand Russell (1872–1970). A man with a mega-brain the size of a lawn-mower, Russell cleverly foresaw the future – in particular, the publication of *The Kenny Everett Ultimate Loo Book*: ' . . . there are two motives for reading a book: one, that you enjoy it, the other that you can boast about it . . .'

May 19th

Many Happy Returns of the day, and a long and happy reign to one of our most brilliant comediennes, Victoria Wood (1953).

TAXI TALES
I was in the back of a London taxi once and saw a notice which made me hoot with laughter. It said: 'Please do not talk to the driver. Nothing you say could possibly interest him . . .'

Which reminds me of a famous story of a politician who suffered a rush-hour crawl through London, listening to the cabbie's stream of bigoted drivel, rubbish and opinionated garbage about the woeful state of the world. Climbing wearily but thankfully from the taxi, the passenger paid the driver off and got his revenge.

'It's such a pity,' he said, 'that all the people who *really* know how to run the world are too busy driving cabs!'

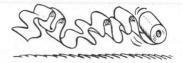

May 20th

And here comes this week's **Astro-loogical Forecast.** Since this book was first published, I've had many letters from people who accuse me of not paying enough attention to Virgo, so just to make up for it, here's the forecast for

CANCER

Don't try to understand the motives of people around you at the moment. Other things not to try include:

a) juggling with rhinoceroses.
b) chewing the rusty bits off Ford Cortinas.
c) confusing Maltesers with rabbit droppings.

Happy Birthday to singer/actress Cher (1945) and to Hollywood Great, James Stewart (1908).

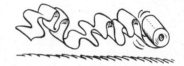

May 21st

Happy Birthday to mega-multi-global bestselling author Harold Robbins (1916), who once proclaimed himself to be the world's greatest writer.

Writing about writing is one of the things writers write about best . . . if you see what I mean. Sample a few of these choice words of wisdom.

'I love being a writer. What I can't stand is the paperwork.' (Peter De Vries)

'Writing is easy; all you do is sit staring at a blank sheet of paper until the drops of blood form on your forehead.' (Gene Fowler)

'There's nothing to writing. All you do is sit down at a typewriter and open a vein.' (Red Smith)

But the final word goes to W. Somerset Maugham: 'There are three rules for writing the novel. Unfortunately, no one knows what they are.'

May 22nd

Happy Birthday to Lord Olivier, thespian-supreme, born in 1907. And I'm sure he'll appreciate this month's **Astroloogical personality profile** for all those born under the sign of

♐ ♑ **GEMINI** ♓ ♊

(May 22nd – June 21st):
Always keen to be everybody's friend, Gemini-born people can never understand why they are so unpopular. Nine times out of ten their lack of popularity is a direct result of the fact that they smell like the north end of a south-bound vulture. Most Geminians live in hope that everything's going to be all right. The rest live in flats or houses.

May 23rd

Many Happy Returns of the day to lip-gloss and shoulder-pads queen Joan Collins (1933). Long may she smoulder!

Today's Loo Laff

Not many people know this, but during the last war there was a secret German training camp located in the middle of the desert. Kommandant Sauerkraut was aware that the trainees – maltreated and ill-fed for a period of several months – were close to breaking point. Mutiny and rebellion lurked around the corner. In order to boost morale, he ordered all the soldiers to assemble under the hot desert sun.

'Vell, men,' he told them, 'there's good news, and there's bad news. Which do you vant to hear first?'

A cry went up from the ranks: 'Ze bad news. Let's get it over with.'

'Well, ze bad news is, all we've got to eat is camel dung.'

'And vot's the good news?' they cried.

'There's plenty of it!'

May 24th

Happy Birthday to comedian Stanley Baxter (1928), and Bob Dylan (1941). And respectful congratulations to Queen Victoria, who was born on this day in 1819 and would now be extremely long in the tooth, had she not popped her right royal clogs in 1901.

LOO-LAW
The scene: a court-room. The cast: a judge, a jury and a defendant.
Defendant: 'Your honour, I wish to plead guilty.'
Judge: 'Why didn't you do so at the beginning of the trial?'
Defendant: Because I thought I was innocent, but at the time I hadn't heard the evidence against me.'

Or, as Robert Frost once said: 'A jury consists of twelve persons chosen to decide who has the better lawyer.'

May 25th

GREAT SPORTING MOMENTS OF OUR TIME – Episode 96

From the department of extraordinary coincidence comes a strange but true tale which happened on this day in 1957.

As you know, the odds against scoring a hole in one are about as great as dissuading a traffic warden from issuing you with a parking ticket. Nonetheless, an actor was playing golf at Richmond golf course in Surrey. He scored a hole in one from the eighth tee. On the same day, a solicitor scored a hole in one from the sixth tee. Nothing too surprising, you may think – except for the fact that both men were named Edward Chapman.

Happy Birthday to American philosopher Ralph Waldo Emerson, a man who obviously suffered at the hand of the critics during his time. He observed that, 'taking to pieces is the trade of those who cannot construct'. The best put-down of critics came from Frank Zappa who said, 'Rock journalism is people who can't write interviewing people who can't talk for people who can't read.' (NB – Personally, I *love* all critics – preferably on toast!)

May 26th

Bathroom Brain-teasers

1 Who were Sophocles' parents?
2 How would you say goodbye to a Japanese?
3 How would you say hello to an estate agent?
4 If King Kong died while playing ping-pong in Hong Kong, where would he be buried?
5 What is the silliest word used by William Shakespeare in one of his plays?

(Answers at foot of page)

Happy Birthday to Robert Morley (1908), a larger-than-life character actor who is clearly very fond of himself: 'I have little patience with anyone who is not self-satisfied. I am always pleased to see my friends, happy to be with my wife and family, but the high-spot of every day is when I first catch a glimpse of myself in the shaving mirror.'

May 27th

Many Happy Returns of the day to singer turned Cupid on 'Blind Date', Cilla Black (1943) and also to Henry Kissinger (1923), the man who claimed that 'power is the ultimate aphrodisiac'. (Obviously he's never tried the old trick with a penguin and a jar of Bovril – more about that in Volume Two!)

Brain-teaser Answers
1) Mr and Mrs Sophocles.   2) Sayonara.   3) Very warily.   4) In a coffin.   5) honorificabilitudinitatibus – in *Love's Labour's Lost*.

Is the door locked? It is? Good. Because I have something very special to impart. Moreover, I want to tell you something. It's this week's Star Forecast, and it's for all those born under the sign of

 **LEO**

You have a certain child-like quality which many people find attractive. You also have a large green bogey dangling from the end of your nose, and are very probably called 'Brian'. If not, please accept my humble apologies, and help yourself to more trifle.

May 28th

Happy Birthday to William Pitt (the Younger), who was born on this day in 1759 and went on to become Prime Minister at the age of 24.

Happy Birthday also to Emilie, Yvonne, Cécile, Marie and Annette Dionne – the world's first known surviving quins, born in Canada on this day in 1937. Five children – can you *imagine*!

When it comes to kids, I don't know a great deal, except that – as an American journalist once wrote – 'the quickest way for a parent to get a child's attention is to sit down and look comfortable.'

Like most people who don't have children of their own, I enjoy the occasional encounter with one of the little people . . . until they get sticky. When that happens, I'm right with Nancy Mitford who said: 'I love children. Especially when they cry – for then someone takes them away.'

May 29th

Many Happy Returns of the day to Bob Hope (1903) – along with George Burns – has some great lines about the advancement of the years. At a party to celebrate his eighty-second birthday, he greeted a galaxy of stars with the words: 'I think it's wonderful you could all be here for the forty-third anniversary of my thirty-ninth birthday. We decided not to light the candles this year – we were afraid Pan Am would mistake it for a runway.'

May 30th

PERFECT PUT-DOWNS:
George Bernard Shaw once invited Winston Churchill to the first night of one of his plays, enclosing two tickets, ' . . . so that you can bring a friend . . . if you have one.' Churchill replied, saying that he was unable to attend the first night, but would be delighted to attend the second, ' . . . if there is one.'

And once at a dinner party, Shaw was pestered by a rather tipsy Socialite beauty: 'We ought to get together and mate. Just imagine a child with my looks and your brains!'

'But, my dear lady,' retorted Shaw wearily, 'think of the disaster if it should turn out the other way round.'

May 31st

Happy Birthday to ex-Mayor of Carmel and sometime actor Clint Eastwood (1930). *Today's Loo Laff*

Two men where travelling on a train.

'Excuse me,' said the first man, 'could you tell me the time!'

No reply.

'I said, excuse me, could you tell me the time?'

Still no reply.

Exasperated, the man raised his voice: 'Would you please tell me what time it is?'

The second man sighed. 'Half-past two.'

'Thank you. And may I ask why you ignored me the first two times I asked . . .?'

'Look, it's like this: you ask me the time, I tell you. We get talking, we become friendly. When we get to my station, I invite you to come for supper with my family. You meet my beautiful daughter. She falls in love with you, and you both want to get married. That's why I didn't answer you the first two times.'

'I don't understand,' said the first man. 'Just supposing that you're right – what would be wrong with that?'

'Well, quite frankly, I don't want my daughter marrying someone who can't afford a watch!'

June 1st

Happy Birthday to Bob Monkhouse (1929) and also to the divine Marilyn Monroe who was born on this day in 1926. Among the many famous stories about Marilyn is the one concerning her first few visits to Arthur Miller's parents. On the first occasion Mrs Miller served matzo balls. Marilyn seemed to enjoy her meal greatly, so when she next came to dinner Mrs Miller served matzo balls again. And the third time . . . and the fourth. On the fifth occasion, Marilyn stared at the plate of food in front of her and turned wearily to her future mother-in-law. 'Gee, Mrs Miller, isn't there any other part of the matzo you can eat?'

June 2nd

Bathroom Brain-teasers

1 Complete the following poem:
   Sir Christopher Wren
   Said, 'I'm going to dine with some men . . .'
2 What is Cliff Richard's real name?
3 What is Kenny Everett's real name?
4 Which of the senses does a dying person normally lose last?
5 What are the names of the rings around Saturn?

(Answers at foot of page)

Brain-teaser Answers

1) ' . . . If anyone calls, Say I'm designing St Paul's. 2) Harry Webb. 3) Maurice Cole! (Can you imagine becoming a world-famous star with a name like Maurice . . .?) 4) Hearing. 5) Ethel, Norman and Algernon.

June 3rd

Happy Birthday to Tony Curtis (1925) who starred with Marilyn Monroe in *Some Like It Hot*. I get the feeling they didn't get on too well; Curtis later said that kissing the world's most famous sex-symbol was 'like kissing Hitler without a moustache'.

It's that time of the month again, folks – and if it's not that time of the month, then it must be this time of the month instead. Above all, it's time for this week's Star Forecast:

♐ ♑ **GEMINI** ♓ ♊

Large amounts of money, exciting new love affairs and foreign travel are all on the cards this week ... but, unfortunately, not for you. In times of adversity, console yourself with the words of the Prophet Tarquin: 'He who breaks a vase before breakfast will break wind before bedtime.'

June 4th

KEEP FIT WITH KEN
(Part 63: exercises for the brain)
  Assume the customary position on the loo.
  Think of a number.
  Double it.
  Add sixty-six.
  Divide by two.
  Subtract ten.
  Multiply by five.
  Subtract another ten.
  Now close your eyes.
  (Dark, innit?)

(Part 64: exercises for the body)

Stand up.

Walk briskly to the living room.

Vigorously unscrew the top of a bottle of whisky.

Jog to the kitchen.

Open the fridge door.

Remove a tray of ice.

Now open the cupboard door and take out a glass.

Prise two ice-cubes from the ice-tray and place them in the glass.

Flexing your biceps, raise the bottle and pour in a large measure of whisky.

Raise the glass to your lips and swallow repeatedly until the glass is empty.

Repeat the exercise until you have the hang of it.

With practice, you should be able to manage five or even six of these in a single day.

June 5th

Happy Birthday to Nigel Rees (1944), novelist and world's champion graffiti-expert. To celebrate, here's a selection of some of my favourites.

JOIN THE ARMY, MEET INTERESTING PEOPLE FROM EXOTIC LANDS . . . AND KILL THEM.

VISIT THE SOVIET UNION . . . BEFORE THE SOVIET UNION VISITS YOU!

GOD IS DEAD
(Oh no, I'm not)

MY DOCTOR SAYS I'M SCHIZOPHRENIC BUT I DON'T BELIEVE HIM AND NEITHER DO I.

BE ALERT! (WE NEED MORE LERTS)

June 6th

PERSONALITY POSERS

Exactly what sort of person are you? Are you a thoroughly princi-pled type? Or are you a lily-livered quivering mass of indecision like the rest of us? Probe the innermost particles of your deepest doobrie, and see how you respond to these Personality Posers:

1 After a splendid meal in a restaurant, you notice that the waitress has *undercharged* you. Do you point out her error, or are you a tight-fisted old nerk?
2 While parking your car, you accidentally scrape the car in front. Do you leave your name and address on the damaged car's windscreen, or are you an anti-social swine?
3 You've planned to see an old friend for dinner, but a more exciting invitation comes your way. What do you do?

(Tricky, aren't they . . .? More later . . .)

June 7th

Happy Birthday to hip-swinging, crotch-gyrating, medallion-draped, burst-sofa-chested Tom Jones (1940). And on this day in 1963 The Rolling Stones made their first-ever television appear-ance on 'Thank Your Lucky Stars'.

The acid-tongued Joan Rivers is obviously a big fan of Mick Jagger's. On a recent TV show she said: 'Mick Jagger has big lips. I saw him suck an egg out of a chicken. He can play a tuba from both ends. This man has got child-bearing lips . . .'

June 8th

Happy Birthday to one of the greatest composers of the century, Cole Porter (1893–1964).

Did you know that stress is one of the largest causes of death in today's world?
See how you score on the Stress-Ometer:

1 You go to the loo in someone else's house and it won't flush. (Score 20 points)
2 You settle down to watch the Bette Davis movie you taped last night, only to discover that the VCR's taped *The Des O'Connor Show* instead. (Score 15 points)
3 You've forgotten that it's your best friend's birthday. Desperately rummaging around in a junk-box, you find one of those mugs that has an unfunny slogan like 'Roses are red, violets are blue-ish; if it wasn't Christmas we'd all be Jewish' printed on it. As your friend is unwrapping it, you suddenly remember he gave it to you last Christmas. (Score 25 points)
4 You're filling in a questionnaire in the Kenny Everett Ultimate Loo Book, when your granny calls to announce she's going to have a sex-change operation. (Score 30 points, and make a fortune by phoning the newspapers)

June 9th

Today's Loo Laff

Q: What does a Jewish Princess make for lunch?
A: Reservations.

Q: How do you know when a Jewish Princess has had an orgasm?
A: She drops her nail-file.

And speaking of matters Royal, did you know that the Queen has her milk delivered in bottles which bear her monogram? Or that when she goes off on a foreign freebie she packs a batch of bangers from Harrods, a jar of mint sauce and several bottles of Malvern water . . . ?

June 10th

Many Happy Returns of the day to Prince Philip (1921), well-known member of the Royal Family who introduced a new word to the English language:

'Dentopedology is the science of opening your mouth and putting your foot in it. I've been practising it for years.'

Yes, it's the page you've been waiting for – here comes this week's **Astro-loogical Forecast**, and it's for

♉ ♊ **TAURUS** ♌ ♎

There's no point in crying over spilt milk, counting your chickens before they go on holiday, or bolting the stable door after the horse has put the cat out for the night. Instead, try counting the number of hairs in Margaret Thatcher's nostrils next time she appears on the box.

June 11th

Uncle Ken's Agony Column

Dear Uncle Ken...

I'd like some advice about my legal rights. I recently had a puncture on account of driving my Range Rover over a milk bottle. This wouldn't be so worrying if the milkman hadn't been holding the bottle at the time. My question is this: am I obliged to leave him a Christmas box this year?

(P.S. The new tyre cost £46.23p, not including VAT.)

Uncle Ken writes:

In my experience, there is little point in crying over spilt milk, and even less point in giving your hard-earned money to milkmen – especially if they're dead and can no longer be relied upon to make regular deliveries.

June 12th

Bathroom Brain-teasers

1 How long can a bed-bug survive without eating?
2 In 1936 Britain had three monarchs – can you name them?
3 What bird's egg is the size of a pea?
4 Why did J. Edgar Hoover never turn left, or allow his driver to do so?
5 Who replaced Roy Plomley as host of 'Desert Island Discs'?

(Answers at foot of page)

On this day in 1965 The Beatles were awarded the MBE in the Birthday Honours List. According to a story which surfaced years later, while the Fab Four were waiting for Her Maj to sock it to them, they sneaked into a loo and smoked one of those naughty cigarettes.

Brain-teaser Answers
1) One year! 2) No. (Oh, all right then: George V, Edward VIII and George VI.) 3) The humming-bird. 4) Because he was so fervently anti-communist. Or, if you prefer, because he was a raving fruit-cake. 5) Michael Parkinson, then Sue Lawley.

June 13th

Happy Birthday to the lady who did more to boost the ratings of my TV show than anybody – the amazingly indomitable Mary Whitehouse (1910).

If you're reading this, Mary, here's a naughty limerick written by that well-known author A. Non.

> An Argentine gaucho named Bruno
> Once said, 'There is something I do know:
> A woman is fine,
> And a sheep is divine,
> But a llama is Numero Uno!'

June 14th

Many Happy Returns to the real Mike Yarwood (1941).

DAFT DEFINITIONS: ONOMATOPOEIA

Impress your friends by using this word in a sentence. The actual dictionary definition is 'a word whose sound fits its sense' – like 'moo' for a cow's words, or 'atchoo' for a sneeze. Or forget being a wise guy and explain onomatopoeia by telling them this joke:

A businessman checked into a New York hotel. While he was taking a bath, he broke wind. Five minutes later a room-service waiter knocks at the door:

'Here's your beer, sir.'

'But . . . I didn't order a beer.'

'How odd,' said the waiter. 'I was in the room below and I could have sworn I heard you call out, "Hey buddy, bring up a bottle of Budweiser."'

June 15th

THE KENNY EVERETT GUIDE TO SURVIVAL IN THE TWENTIETH CENTURY

(and how to avoid being pestered by people who drive you bananas):

Next time someone you can't stand telephones to invite you to a party you don't want to go to, take a leaf out of John Barrymore's book. Asked to attend a boring dinner party, Barrymore declined, saying, 'I'm afraid I have a previous engagement, which I shall make the moment you put the phone down.'

June 16th

Belated congratulations to Andrew Jackson who, on this day in 1903, patented the world's first eyeglasses . . . for chickens.

I love eccentrics – especially on toast. One of my favourite fruit-cakes was a king of Persia called Khosru the Second who did a spot of ruling in the fifth century. He was so into showing off that whenever he went on a royal walkabout, a thousand slaves watered the roads ahead of him, followed by another two hundred who scattered perfumes in his path.

June 17th

Happy Birthday to Super-Schnozz Barry Manilow (1946) and the delightfully dippy Beryl Reid (1920).

Would **you like to know** how to get rich, **how to meet** beautiful people, **and how to** live happily ever **after. You** would? Well, that's **two of us.**

In the meantime, here's your

Star Forecast for the coming week:

♈ ♓ ♌ **LEO** ♉ ♊ ♋

There is a lot to be said for keeping yourself to yourself at the moment. There's also a lot to be said for keeping weasels in the turn-ups of your trouser pockets, although this is unlikely to provide such a good return on your investment. Your lucky colour is blue ... with a dash of tangerine and a yellow polka-dot stripe down the middle.

June 18th

Two of this century's greatest songwriters were born on this day, so **Happy Birthday** to Sammy Cahn (1913) and Paul McCartney (1942).

Today's Loo Laff

All of high society turned out for the charity ball in aid of the Royal Society for the Prevention of Cruelty to Houseplants. A young down-and-out 'Hooray Henry' was very taken with the glittering sight of a massive diamond ring on the finger of a middle-aged woman.

'What a sensational gem,' he breathed in her ear. 'Do tell me about it.'

'This?' said the woman. 'Oh, this is the famous Zelnick diamond. Beautiful, isn't it? Unfortunately, it has a curse attached to it.'

'A curse, how fascinating! What curse?'

'*Mr* Zelnick.'

June 19th

INVENTOR'S CORNER

On this day in 1896, a Russian **nobleman** invented the world's first safety coffin. If someone **was buried** by mistake, the slightest movement inside the coffin **would set a** bell ringing, a flag waving and light up a lamp. There **was** also a speaking tube which connected the unfortunate **not-so-stiff** stiff with the surface.

June 20th

Bathroom Brain-teasers

1 Which country, per capita, owns the most umbrellas?
2 Why do we shiver?
3 A fortieth anniversary is Ruby – what is a third anniversary?
4 On what type of substance is the Mona Lisa painted?
5 How long does an average snowflake take to fall from 1,000 feet?

(Answers at foot of page)

Happy Birthday to hell-raising actor Errol Flynn (1909–1959) who lived life to the full, and confessed that his problem lay in '... trying to reconcile my gross habits with my net income'. He also said, 'Any man who has $10,000 left when he dies is a failure.'

Brain-teaser Answers

1) England. 2) Because shivering increases the muscular activity, and therefore raises the body's temperature – clever, eh? 3) Leather. 4) Wood. 5) Between 8 and 10 minutes.

June 21st

Many Happy Returns of the day to Prince William of Wales (1982). Searching through the files for his most famous quotes to date, I came across the following memorable statement: 'Goo bur boo boo glunge squart . . .' And who's going to argue with that? Being a loyal subject, I'd like to wish His Extreme Gorgeousness all sorts of good fortune, and may the bluebird of happiness fly up his nose for ever.

June 22nd

Happy Birthday to one of the few mega-box-office stars of the Eighties, the dynamically wonderfully brilliantly marvellously multi-talented Meryl Streep (1949) who may be interested in her **Astro-loogical personality profile** which applies to all those born under the sign of

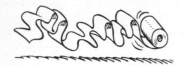

♋♊ CANCER ♉♌

(June 22nd – July 23rd)
It is very common for Cancerians to be visited by a plague of fleas and headlice. It is even more common for them to be visited by relations from Bournemouth and, given the choice, they'd pick the fleas any day. Cancerians are known to be extremely fond of children, animals and pickled onions.

June 23rd

BEDTIME STORIES:
Next time you're having trouble nodding off, consider these Fascinating Facts:

On average, men sleep for eight hours a night; women sleep for twenty minutes longer. Men tend to snore more than women, which just goes to prove the old adage: 'Men tend to snore more than women.'

Our dreams tend to take up one and three quarter hours a night – longer if Whitney Houston is involved. And – don't ask me how – but sleep is a great way of losing weight: on average, we lose 1lb a night!

June 24th

Here's another fascinating fact – exclusive to readers of *The Kenny Everett Ultimate Loo Book:* today is the only day of the year when the date will be *exactly* the same as it was on this date last year ... While you're working that out, work out this week's **Astro-loogical Forecast**:

♎ ♋ **LIBRA** ♌ ♍

With Mars, Pluto and Jupiter currently entering Neptune, Neptune's getting pretty busy at the moment and is on the look-out for larger premises. Your lucky carpet is Axminster Special Weave.

June 25th

Today's the anniversary of Custer's Last Stand at the Battle of the Little Big Horn in 1876. A historical footnote to the battle reveals that Custer didn't have much faith in his chances of survival: he took the precaution of insuring himself for $5,000 before the battle.

LAWS OF THE UNIVERSE:
Murphy's Law: If anything can go wrong, it will.
O'Toole's Commentary on Murphy's Law:– Murphy was an optimist.
Jenning's Corollary: The chance of bread falling with the buttered side up is directly proportional to the cost of the carpet.
Everett's Corollary to Jenning's Corollary: Bread will always fall buttered side up – unless you are trying to demonstrate Jenning's Corollary.

June 26th

Do you sometimes feel like a failure? Does the world fail to recognise your genius? Well, don't be down-hearted. Even the most successful people have had their failures:
The original M.A.S.H. book was turned down by twenty-one publishers, and eighteen more passed up the chance to publish *Lorna Doone*.

And even the most successful companies make mistakes. A well-known American bed manufacturer spent a fortune and invested four years' effort exporting beds to Japan. It was only after the fourth year that they realised the fundamental flaw in their marketing policy: the Japanese don't sleep on beds, they prefer futons. So, just remember the old saying: 'If at first you don't succeed, try, try, try again. If you *still* don't succeed, give up – you're obviously a schmuck.'

June 27th

Many Happy Returns of the day to Alan Coren (1938), former *Punch* editor and TV critic who once wrote in *The Times*: 'Television is more interesting than people. If it were not, we should have people standing in the corner of our rooms.'

Today's Loo Laff

Another example of the wonderful Jewish sense of humour:
Morris Goldberg was having dinner in a Chinese restaurant when the waiter accidentally spilled some soya sauce on his shirt.

'You blasted Japanese!' yelled Morris. 'First Pearl Harbor, now this!'

'Actually, sir,' replied the waiter, 'I'm not Japanese, I'm Chinese.'

'Chinese, Japanese . . . so what's in a name?'

'Anyway,' said the waiter, 'you Jews – you can talk! You sank the *Titanic*!'

'Don't be ridiculous,' said Morris. 'The *Titanic* was sunk by an iceberg.'

'Iceberg, Goldberg . . . so what's in a name?'

June 28th

Bathroom Brain-teasers

1 Which **pocket** does a pickpocket find it easiest to pick?
2 According to the tongue-twister, what noise annoys a noisy oyster most?
3 What is the main ingredient of glass?
4 Which of the body's muscles can work for the longest without getting tired?
5 How much sweat does the average pair of feet give off daily?

(Answers at foot of page)

Happy Birthday to Liberal politican and butt of many jokes, Cyril Smith (1928).

Brain-teaser Answers

1) The breast-pocket. 2) A noisy noise annoys a noisy oyster most. 3) Sand. 4) The jaw muscles (cf: Gyles Brandreth). 5) Half a pint (cf: Gyles Brandreth).

June 29th

THE
KENNY EVERETT
GUIDE TO SURVIVAL IN THE
TWENTIETH CENTURY

(and how to get through the day without an attack of the screaming ab-dabs)
(Part 68676303955)

1 When peeling an onion, hold it under water to avoid the fumes.

2 When trying to loosen a stubborn screw-top jar, wrap an elastic band around the top for extra grip.

3 To stop birds pecking at your milk-bottle tops, issue your milkman with a Thompson submachine-gun.

4 To stop your pet from making nasty messes on the carpet, don't give it anything to eat or drink.

June 30th

WHAT A SWELL PARTY THAT WAS ...!

The birthday party of the century took place on this day in 1905, hosted by an American millionaire called George Kessler. He arranged for the courtyard of the Savoy Hotel to be flooded, and had his guests all seated in gondolas. The birthday cake made a spectacular entrance on the back of an elephant. The only thing which marred the occasion was the death of the specially imported swans which were supposed to swim around the place – they were poisoned by the blue dye in the water.

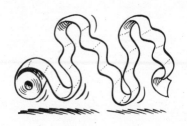

July 1st

Happy Birthday to HRH The Princess of Wales, who did one of the best gags of the century when she pretended to forget her husband's name just as they were about to get hitched. (Who writes this woman's material?)

Charles Darwin first announced his Theory of Evolution on this day in 1858. At first people found it difficult to believe that we were descended from apes, and it wasn't until Oliver Reed was born in 1938 that everyone began to take Darwin really seriously.

Time to peek into the future and see what exciting surprises the fickle finger of fate has in store for you this week, especially if you were born under the sign of

CANCER

If someone dear to you has been feeling a little under the weather recently, try showing them some extra care and compassion. If this fails, try showing them your collection of celebrity nostril-hair.

July 2nd

Happy Birthday to Dr David Owen (1938).

HELPFUL HINTS ON HOW TO SURVIVE PARTIES;

a) Always take your own car.

b) Always take your own supply of phlegm.

c) Only give guests a drink if they agree to juggle with their eyeballs.

d) In the middle of the *boeuf en croute à la Marseillaise,* reveal your hidden store of knowledge about flatworms – a rare breed of animal which reproduce by pulling themselves to pieces; each part then develops into a worm.

I promise, it'll be a party no one will forget!

July 3rd

Bathroom Brain-teasers

1 For what purpose were Kleenex tissues originally manufactured?
2 Which famous playwright celebrates his birthday on the same day every year? (Clue somewhere on this page.)
3 Translate 'Veni, Vidi, Vici'.
4 Translate 'Veni, Vidi, Visa'.
5 By how many is the human population of Australia outnumbered by sheep?

(Answers at foot of page)

Happy Birthday to playwright and philosopher Tom Stoppard (1937). Characters in his plays always say such great things, like these two quotes from *Rosencrantz And Guildenstern Are Dead*:

'Life is a gamble at terrible odds – if it was a bet, you wouldn't take it.'

'Eternity is a terrible thought. I mean, where's it going to end?'

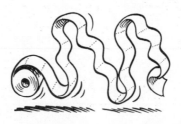

Brain-teaser Answers

1) Gas-mask filters during World War One.   2) Yes, it's Tom Stoppard. Also celebrating on the same day every year are every other playwright ever born.   3) I came, I saw, I conquered.   4) I came, I saw, I went shopping.   5) Ten to one.

July 4th

And **Many Happy Returns** of the day to American playwright Neil Simon (1927) who wrote *The Odd Couple,* a movie which bursts at the seams with fab lines like the description of a very uptight, nervous person: 'The only man in the world with clenched hair.'

The American Declaration of Independence was signed on 4 July in 1776, and by strange coincidence the second and third US Presidents both snuffed it on this day in 1826. This just goes to prove something about July 4th, but I'm not terribly sure what.

July 5th

Today's Loo Laff

A well-connected pair of honeymooners had been lent a very grand country house for their first week as man and wife. On the third day, the bride finally got out of bed and went down to the vast kitchens where she prepared breakfast for her new husband. She took the tray up to the bedroom, proudly displaying a silver salver of bacon and eggs, surrounded by a bed of lettuce.

'Darling, how wonderful,' said the man. 'But what's all the lettuce for?'

'Oh,' she said, 'I wanted to see if you also *eat* like a rabbit.'

July 6th

Happy Birthday to comedian Dave Allen (1936) and to Nancy Reagan, wife of one of the greatest comics of all time. Robin Williams once observed, 'I still think Nancy does most of his talking; you'll notice that she *never* drinks water when Ronnie speaks.' And Steve Martin (the funniest man in the history of funniest men) said; 'I believe that Ronald Reagan can make this country what it once was – an arctic region covered with ice.'

July 7th

Many Happy Returns of the day to Ringo Starr (1940) who's a sausage-pie sweetheart of the first order, even if he's never too sure what's going on: 'Do you remember when everybody began analysing Beatle songs? I don't think I understood what some of them were supposed to be about.'

THE
KENNY EVERETT
GUIDE TO SURVIVAL IN THE
TWENTIETH CENTURY

(and how to avoid unnecessary stains on the lino):

Never scrape all your skin off the Brillo pad unless you keep a spare under the bed.

July 8th

Are you feeling nervous, tired, worried about the future? Well, so am I, so let's put our minds at rest by seeing what's in store for those delightful, charming people – like me – born under the sign of

CAPRICORN

Try not to let minor irritations get under your skin this weekend. Collect them carefully in a Tupperware container and send them to NATO headquarters in Helsinki. Once they have arrived safely, they will be turned into intercontinental ballistic lemon sherbets.

Happy Birthday to John D. Rockerfeller (1839–1937). In the course of his lifetime he donated over $500m to charity. (Rumour has it that you *can* buy your way into heaven after all. Recent reports indicate that Rockerfeller's cloud has an avocado bathroom suite, and hot and cold running cherubim and seraphim.)

July 9th

Happy Birthday to the world's pinkest person and most prolific writer, Barbara Cartland (1901).

FAIRLY FASCINATING FACTS ABOUT BARBARA CARTLAND;

1 When TV crews go to her home to interview her, she has a special room set aside where the lighting is always designed to make her look good.
2 Since you started reading this page, Barbara Cartland has written seven new books. Prolific just isn't the word! (In fact the word is 'squelch' – well done if you spotted it.)

July 10th

Five facts you never knew before and will probably never ever need to know unless you get stuck in a lift with a member of the R.S.P.C.M. (Royal Society for Prevention of Cruelty to Mayonnaise):

1 Crocodiles are unable to stick out their tongues.
2 If you meet a Masai warrior on the tube, spit at him – it's considered a sign of politeness and respect.
3 During the first year of his marriage to Jackie Kennedy, Aristotle Onassis spent approximately $20,000,000 on gifts for her.
4 In order to safeguard her secrets, the Queen uses black ink and black blotting paper.
5 The Russian word for God is *Bog*.

July 11th

Bathroom Brain-teasers

1 How many cups of tea does the average Englishman drink each year?
2 What is everyone saying behind your back?
3 Where was Magna Carta signed?
4 What is the original meaning of the word 'bride'?
5 Why is the racoon one of the fussiest animals in the world?

(Answers at foot of page)

July 12th

Many Happy Returns of the day to American comedian Milton Berle (1908), whose marriage went through a sticky patch a while ago:

'The other night I said to my wife Ruth, "Do you feel that the sex and excitement has gone out of our marriage?" Ruth said, "I'll discuss it with you during the next commercial."'

Berle's also a great fan of game-shows: 'A woman won a vacation and dropped dead from the shock, but the sponsors kept their word. They sent her body to Bermuda for two weeks.'

Brain-teaser Answers

1) 2,000. 2) *a)* your feet smell; *b)* you're a lush; *c)* nothing; you're too dull to be a topic of conversation. 3) All together now: 'At the bottom.' Boom boom! 4) To cook (old Teutonic word). 5) Because it washes its food before eating it.

July 13th

Happy Birthday to Harrison 'Indiana Jones' Ford (1942).

Today's Loo Laff

In a desperate attempt to stop her little daughter from biting her nails, Mrs Spong said: 'If you carry on doing that, you'll get a big fat tummy.'

The following week they were on a train, and Mrs Spong pointed to an enormously fat man. 'Look,' she whispered. 'Now *there's* a man who bites his nails if ever I saw one.'

At the next station, an extremely pregnant woman boarded the train. The little girl stared intently at her for what seemed like an eternity.

'Why are you staring at me like that?' asked the woman. 'Do you know me?'

'No,' said the little girl, 'but I know what you've been up to.'

July 14th

Uncle Ken's Agony Column

Dear Uncle Ken...

I want to ask your advice about my wife. She's a woman of rare gifts – in fact, she hasn't given me a present for twenty-five years. Her mother is the one who really gets my goat. Last week, I cut my finger and she burst into tears. At first I took this as a display of affection, but she later revealed that she was only trying to get some salt into the wound. I have recently fallen in love with my secretary, the delightful Letitia Leftover. Divorce from my present wife is simply not on. My question is this: under British law, what is the maximum penalty for bigamy?

Uncle Ken writes

Two mothers-in-law.

July 15th

This week's fantastically fortunate forecast is for:

♉ ♊ TAURUS ♌ ♎

In spite of what people have been telling you recently, there is no need to be frightened of low-flying Chinese waiters. You will be perfectly safe, as long as your underwear contains no more than three artificial preservatives. Your lucky number is green, and your lucky corpse is Al Jolson.

July 16th

PERSONALITY POSERS:
Are you man, or mouse? Woman, or worm? Find out by asking yourself these unanswerable questions:

1 You're a guest in someone's house and your cigarette actually burns your host's new sofa. No one notices. Do you own up? And do you make a good *spaghetti alle vongole*?
2 You discover that your closest friend is a Russian spy. Do you *a)* turn him into the nearest policeman? *b)* turn him into a life-size model of Joan Collins?
3 It's wartime and you're captured by the enemy and interrogated. The boss of the interrogators is a dead ringer for Bo Derek/Harrison Ford. What is your favourite toothpaste?

July 17th

Happy Birthday to ex-Goodie Tim Brooke Taylor (1940), James Cagney (1899) and American comedienne Phyllis Diller who revealed her *Housekeeping Hints* to the world:
    'Cleaning your house while your kids are growing is like shovelling the walk before it stops snowing.'
    As for relationships, she had this piece of advice: 'Never go to bed mad. Stay up and fight!'

July 18th

Happy Birthday to condomking and boss of the Virgin Empire, Richard Branson (1950).

Which reminds me of two little boys who were overheard by their teacher:'

'I found a condom on the patio,' said the first.

'Really,' said his friend. 'What's a patio?'

THE
KENNY EVERETT
GUIDE TO SURVIVAL IN THE
TWENTIETH CENTURY

(Part 8712436476248768861)

Never try to exist on a diet which consists solely of deeppile carpet and rusty hinges.

July 19th

Bathroom Brain-teasers

1 Approximately what percentage of the world's population uses a knife and fork at mealtimes?
2 How many teeth does a tortoise have?
3 How many dwarfs are there in *Snow White and the Seven Dwarfs*?
4 What is a group of swine called?
5 What do you get if you cross an elephant with a peanut-butter sandwich?

(Answers at foot of page)

Brain-teaser Answers

1) One third. 2) None. 3) Don't be silly. 4) A sounder, or a drift. 5) Either a sandwich that never forgets, or an elephant that sticks to the roof of your mouth.

July 20th

On this day in 1969, Neil Armstrong landed on the Moon and became the first man to boldly go where no hand has ever set foot.

Five Fascinating Facts to pass the time when you're next on a long-distance ardvaark to Cairo:

1 In the eighteenth century, parents used to quieten teething babies by rubbing a hare's brain on their gums. (I think that would shut up kids in any century, don't you?)
2 The male silkworm moth's sense of smell is so acute that he can sniff out a female silkworm moth five miles away.
3 Bernard Manning's mind is so filthy that he can sniff out a dirty joke at a distance of twenty miles, even if his nose is submerged in camel-dung.
4 Instead of wearing nappies, Chinese babies have a hole cut in their trousers.
5 Every baby that ever sits on my lap relieves itself within 3.6 seconds.

July 21st

Today's Loo Laff

The vicar called to take tea with an old spinster whose only company was a talking parrot. The vicar noticed that the bird had a red string tied around its left leg, and a green string tied around its right leg.

'What are those strings for?' enquired the vicar.

'Ah,' said the old lady. 'If I pull the red string he sings *Onward Christian Soldiers,* and if I pull the green one he sings *Silent Night.*'

'How fascinating,' said the vicar. 'And what happens if you pull both at the same time?'

'I fall off my bleedin' perch, you daft old sod!' screeched the parrot.

July 22nd

Hello, loo-lovers! Yes, once again it's Star Time . . .

♐ ♑ **GEMINI** ♓ ♊

A week when you should try to avoid getting involved in other people's arguments. You should also avoid treading in nasty brown messes left on the pavement by dogs. There is a chance that you will be forced to auction your collection of waterproof lemmings, but be of good cheer and remember – start off every day with a smile, and get it over with.

July 23rd

The first-ever Olympic Games opened at Olympia in the Peloponnese on this day in 776BC.

Although I've been known to bash the living daylights out of the occasional squash ball (I always pretend it's a VAT inspector), I'm not one of life's great sporting heroes. In fact, I go along with American writer Fran Lebowitz who said: 'When it comes to sports I am not particularly interested. Generally speaking, I look upon them as dangerous and tiring activities performed by people with whom I share nothing except the right to trial by jury.'

July 24th

Astro-loogical personality profile for all those born under the sign of

♈ ♓ ♌ **LEO** ♉ ♊ ♋

(July 24th – August 23rd): Leo-born people are well-known for their high-cheekbones, their ability as peace-makers, and their extremely weak bladders. Many a delicate diplomatic negotiation has been interrupted to answer a call of nature. (Some diplomatic negotiations have been interrupted for the sake of sending out for cheeseburgers and a bevvy of dancing girls, but that's a different story.)

July 25th

Happy Birthday to Louise Brown – the world's first test-tube baby, born on this day in 1978.

Other Potty Pioneers include Alan Andrew of Wales, who set the world record for lying on a bed of sharp nails – 273 hours (nearly eleven and a half days!). For the final 34 hours, his fiancée Katherine Weston joined him on the bed of nails. History does not record how they spent their honeymoon night.

And hats off to a man called Frank Watts who once wrote the Lord's Prayer 34 times on the back of a regular-sized British postage stamp!

July 26th

Happy Birthday to Mick Jagger (1943). And also to George Bernard Shaw (1856–1950), who probably said more great things than anyone else in the history of people who say really great things. Here are just a few of his *bons mots*:

'When a stupid man is doing something he is ashamed of, he always declares that it is his duty.'

'A drama critic is a man who leaves no turn unstoned.'

'The ideal love affair is conducted by post.'

'Alcohol is a very necessary article . . . It enables Parliament to do things at eleven at night that no sane person would do at eleven in the morning.'

July 27th

Bathroom Brain-teasers

1 If you eat something *en croute* what would it be like?
2 If you eat something *en concrete,* where would you go after your meal?
3 Legally speaking, when is 'time immemorial'?
4 On which Shakespeare play is the musical *West Side Story* based?
5 Is it wise for a man with a lisp to wear a pith-helmet?

(Answers at foot of next page)

Happy Birthday to champion ice-skater Christopher Dean (1958).

July 28th

Happy Birthday to Jackie Onassis (1929).

As this book is custom-built for reading in the 'smallest room', I thought you should know all there is to know about one of the most fascinating subjects in the entire world; yes, it's KENNY EVERETT'S exclusive on Loo Rolls . . .!

The average family in Britain uses 90 rolls of lavatory paper every year, which works out at approximately two miles – enough to amuse 62.3 cute little puppies until the cows come home. And spare a thought for those tireless workers in the armed services and the civil service who have to 'rough it' in more ways than one. According to Her Majesty's Stationery Office, the armed forces and civil servants are issued with two thousand million sheets of nasty, scratchy loo paper every year. That's 180,000 miles – almost enough to reach the moon! If soft loo paper were used instead, the taxpayers (that's you and me) would have to stump up for an extra half-million pounds per anus . . . sorry, *per annum.*

July 29th

Over half-way through the year – and what a year it is: every month packed with weeks, every day filled with hours, and every minute brimming over with seconds. While you're working that one out, here's this week's Star Forecast, and it's for

♏ SCORPIO ♐

A disagreement with a friend will lead to a major depression this evening. This will give way to sunny spells, scattered showers and a large boil on your backside. It's not often that you get invited to appear naked on prime-time television, and this week is no exception.

July 30th

Happy Birthday to Daley Thompson and Kate Bush, both born in 1958 (but not to the same parents).

Today's Loo Laff

An absent-minded man finally remembered that he had an appointment with the doctor.

'My problem is,' he said, 'that I'm unbelievably forgetful. I just keep forgetting things.'

'Really?' said the doctor. 'How disturbing for you. And how long has this been going on?'

The man frowned. 'How long has *what* been going on?'

Brain-teaser Answers

1) Enveloped in pastry. 2) To the dentist. 3) Before the reign of Richard I (1189–1199). 4) *Romeo and Juliet.* 5) Thertainly not.

July 31st

On this day in 1910, mass murderer Dr Crippen was arrested for the murder of his wife. He was apprehended on board the S.S. *Montrose* just before she docked in Quebec. This was the first time wireless telegraphy had been used to help capture a criminal.

THE KENNY EVERETT GUIDE TO SURVIVAL IN THE TWENTIETH CENTURY

If you're a compulsive nail-biter, try this simple remedy: remove your fingers and keep them out of reach until such time as you *really* need them.

August 1st

Happy Birthday to fashion supremo Yves St Laurent (1936). It's amazing how much bitchiness is inspired by fashion. The old snob's rule about so-called 'designer' clothes is that, 'if you matter, you don't mind; and if you mind, you don't matter.' But let's see what good old Fran Lebowitz has to say on the subject: 'While clothes with pictures and/or writing on them are not entirely an invention of the modern age, they are an unpleasant indication of the general state of things . . I mean, be realistic. If people don't want to listen to *you*, what makes you think they want to hear from your sweater?'

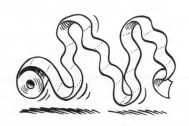

August 2nd

Happy Birthday to Peter O'Toole (1932) and Alan Whicker who's been trotting around the globe since 1925.

It's said that travel broadens the mind, and the subject certainly exercised the grey matter of the readers of *New Statesman* magazine some years ago when they were asked to supply UNHELPFUL ADVICE FOR FOREIGN TOURISTS;

1 On first entering an Underground train, it is customary to shake hands with every passenger.
2 Women are not allowed upstairs on buses; if you see a woman there, ask her politely to descend.
3 Most foreign tourists know that in London they are encouraged to take a piece of fruit, free of charge, from any open-air stall or display.

August 3rd

Many Happy Returns of the day to Tony Bennett, who's somehow managed to survive since 1926, in spite of the fact that his heart got lost on the West Coast of America. And **Happy Birthday** to Terry Wogan, who was born on this day in 1938.

Today's Loo Laff

A couple of old-aged pensioners decided to celebrate their fiftieth anniversary by returning to the country hotel where they had spent their honeymoon.

'Ah,' said the old lady, 'this brings back such happy memories. Do you remember how eager you were to make love to me. You were so impatient – you didn't even give me time to take off my stockings.'

'Well,' replied her husband, 'you needn't worry tonight. You'll have time to knit yourself a pair.'

August 4th

Bathroom Brain-teasers

1 What is the capital of Yugoslavia?
2 What is the capital of Edwina Currie?
3 By what ratio do right-handed people outnumber left-handed people?
4 Whose last words were 'Die, my dear doctor? That's the last thing I shall do'?
5 What is the difference between lamb and mutton?

(Answers at foot of page)

A very **Happy Birthday** to everyone's favourite royal – the Queen Mum who's as old as the century. Her advice to anyone about to marry into the family and become a Royal Personage is, 'Never miss an opportunity to use a loo.'

Brain-teaser Answers

1) Belgrade. 2) You're just being silly again. 3) Five to One. 4) Lord Palmerston. 5) Mutton refers to sheep over twelve months old.

August 5th

In times of self-doubt we all turn to the stars to see what fate has in store for us, and to-day is no exception. Here comes this week's **Astro-loogical Forecast**, and it's for

♈ ♓ ♌ **LEO** ♉ ♊ ♋

You will be viewed as the fount of all wisdom this week when you discover the answer to the age-old question: How much is that doggie in the window? In the words of Saint Wendy the Insatiable, 'It is easier for a camel to pass through the eye of a needle than it would be for a banana to change the oil fil-ter on a Ford Sierra.' And who can argue with that . . . ?

August 6th

Many Happy Returns of the day to Lucille Ball (1910), Amer-ica's favourite comedienne. Also to Hollywood tough guy, Robert Mitchum (1917). Years ago Mitchum was a guest on Michael Parkinson's chat show; renowned for being monosyllabic, he answered each of Parky's questions with a simple 'Yup', or 'Nope'.

Exasperated, Parkinson asked, 'With your tough-guy image, do people come up to you and try to pick fights?'

'Nope,' said Mitchum. Parkinson sat there, leaving the syllable hanging in mid-air while the studio audience bristled with ten-sion.

After a pause, Mitchum leaned forward. 'There was one occa-sion,' he said, 'when I was insulted by a guy in a bar. I decided to teach him some manners . . .' (At this point, Parkinson sat for-ward, sensing a good story on the way.) 'So,' drawled Mitchum, 'I got a fork and I grabbed the back of the guy's head, forcing the prongs of the fork up through his nostrils until the blood was spurting all over the place. That's how I deal with people like him.'

Boggle-eyed, Parkinson breathed, 'You're kidding!'

'Yup,' said Mitchum, deadpan.

August 7th

Many Happy Returns of the day to super-spy, Mata Hari (1876-1917), and **Happy Birthday** (sort of) to the Daylight Saving Act which was passed on this day in 1925, invented to deprive us poor, hardworking Britons of an hour of sleep every year. Like everyone else, I find the whole business of putting my clocks backwards and forwards terribly confusing. By the time I've raced around the house re-setting the alarm clock, the video clock, the kitchen clock, the cuckoo clock, my watch, the grandfather clock, the bathroom clock, the coal-cellar clock . . . a whole year has passed and it's time to wind them all the other way. Bureaucrats! Don'cha hate 'em . . . ?

August 8th

Happy Birthday to Dustin Hoffman (1937) who – although he's a brilliant actor – has a reputation for being somewhat difficult to get along with. Larry Gelbart, who wrote *Tootsie*, once said that his experiences with Dustin Hoffman taught him one very valuable lesson: 'Never work with an Oscar-winning star who's shorter than the statue itself.'

PHILOSOPHICAL STATEMENT OF THE DAY
'He who laughs last laughs loudest.'
 Or
'He who laughs last probably hasn't understood the joke.'

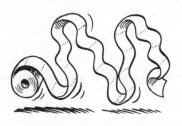

August 9th

BATTLE OF THE SEXES (Department of Mothers-in-Law):
Of all the topics which provide gag material, mothers-in-law must come top of the list. So I make no apologies for presenting a few of the best-ever jokes on the subject. Les Dawson is, of course, king of the in-law baiters: 'Every Christmas the wife's mother has been coming to our house for dinner. This year we're having a change: we're going to let her in.'

Definition of mixed emotion: watching your mother-in-law drive off a cliff in your new car.

And then there was Morecambe and Wise's famous line:
    'She went on and on about it.'
    'And did you give her as good as you got?'
    'Of course – I gave her a really good listening to.'

August 10th

Use your time wisely: test your moral courage with these PERSONALITY POSERS:
1 A doctor confides in you, telling you that your best friend has a terrible disease – one which means losing the faculty to differentiate between Stork margarine and Alan Whicker's nasal hair. Do you withold this devastating news, or do you place an advertisement in *The Times*, telling the world about your friend's misfortune?
2 While cat-sitting for your holidaying neighbour, the animal is run over by a steam-roller. Do you *a*) come clean and break the news to your neighbours, or *b*) make the cat's coat into a pair of gloves and present it to them on their return as a form of consolation?

August 11th

Today's Loo Laff

If anyone ever asks you what 'one-up-manship' means, tell them this story:

Two boys hated each other all through their schooldays. One went on to become an admiral, the other a bishop. Just before their retirement they were both invited to travel to London for a reception at Buckingham Palace – full ceremonial dress was the order of the day. The admiral was wearing his cocked hat, and the bishop – by now a very fat chappie – was clad in his skirt-like black cloak and gaiters.

Recognising his old rival on the station platform, the bishop went up to the admiral. 'Excuse me porter, what time is the train for London?'

The admiral immediately cottoned on to the game and replied, 'At two-thirty, madam. But in your present advanced state, I would advise you not to travel.'

August 12th

In the midst of all this madness, it's good to know there's something you can rely on: good old fate – so let's see what she has in store for us this week. It's the turn of

♎ ♋ LIBRA ♌ ♍

Few people understand the troubles you've been through over the last few weeks, and fewer still understand the Theory of Relativity. Consequently you can expect little sympathy from anyone of foreign extraction. You can also expect to run out of cream crackers much earlier than anticipated. Your lucky item of office furniture is the filing cabinet.

August 13th

Happy Birthday to John Logie Baird (1888–1946) who invented television, **thus** ensuring that the likes of li'l ol' me had something to **do when** they grew up.

And **from the** Department of Biting the Hand that Feeds you come **David Frost's** thoughts on the subject of television: '. . . an invention **that permits** you to be entertained in your living-room by people **you wouldn't** have in your home.'

August 14th

Bathroom Brain-teasers

1 At what age can you marry in France?
2 What do you get if you cross a chicken with a banjo?
3 If two Bishops are in bed, which one will wear the nightie?
4 What is Margaret Thatcher's middle name?
5 Which classic book opens with the words, 'It was a bright cold day in April and the clocks were striking thirteen . . .'

(Answers at foot of page)

THE
KENNY EVERETT
GUIDE TO SURVIVAL IN THE
TWENTIETH CENTURY

When dealing with poultry, it's always wise to pluck the chicken before the chicken plucks you.

Brain-teaser Answers

1) Fifteen.   2) A self-plucking chicken.   3) Mrs Bishop.
4) Hilda.   5) *1984* by George Orwell.

August 15th

Happy Birthday to Princess Anne (1950), who greatly endeared herself to millions when she told a group of interfering reporters to 'Naff Orf'.

Napoleon's also celebrating a birthday today (1769–1821) and so is T.E. Lawrence – better known as Lawrence of Arabia (1888–1935). When Lawrence was in the R.A.F., he once received a letter from Noël Coward which began: 'Dear 338171 (May I call you 338) . . .'

August 16th

On this day in 1977, Elvis Presley died. He was once reported to have said, 'I don't know anything about music. In my line you don't have to.'

Uncle Ken's Agony Column

Dear Uncle Ken...

I am writing in desperation about my husband. He has recently developed an insane belief that he is a talented man – a born entertainer for whom show business is calling. Last week, he tried out his new act at our local Conservative Association's Summer Ball. He does impressions of farmyard animals. In itself, this is not so worrying except that he doesn't do the noises, he does the smells. What shall I do?

Uncle Ken writes:

It's good for a man to have a hobby. Instead of criticising him, why don't you join in the fun? Think of all the good times you could have, putting on shows for the family at Christmas-time. My only recommendation is that you should consider taking your show to outdoor arenas.

August 17th

Happy Birthday to Robert de Niro (1943) and dear old Mae West (1892–1980) who had squillions of funny lines attributed to her, like:

'Is that a gun in your pocket or are you just pleased to see me?'

'Marriage is a great institution, but I'm not ready for an institution.'

'It's not the men in my life, but the life in my men that counts.'

And in the 1932 film *Night After Night*, someone remarked on her gems, 'Goodness, what beautiful diamonds!' Mae retorted, 'Goodness had nothing to do with it, dearie.'

August 18th

The uncanny resemblance between Robert Redford and Willie Rushton can be explained by the fact that they were both born on this day in 1937. And the much-married Shelley Winters is also celebrating her birthday today (1922). 'I did a picture in England one winter,' she said, 'and it was so cold I almost got married.' 'In Hollywood all marriages are happy. It's trying to live together afterwards that causes all the problems.'

THOUGHT FOR THE DAY

Death is life's answer to the question, 'Why?'

August 19th

I've been gazing deep into my crystal ball again, dear reader, and I've come up with what promises to be a very exciting week for

♏ **SCORPIO** ↗

There's a lot of explaining to do when a friend lets the cat out of the bag, and you will be clawed to ribbons to get the wretched thing back in. A tricky situation may call for you to lie through your teeth. If this fails, try lying through your nostrils. (NB: Medical fact: it is much easier to brush your teeth than to brush your nostrils.)

August 20th

Today's Loo Laff

A wartime spiv failed his medical test on the grounds that he couldn't read the optician's chart. The eye specialist was suspicious to say the least, but was forced to classify him as unfit for active service.

That evening, the specialist went to the cinema and was outraged to see the spiv with his arm around a pretty young girl, laughing his head off at the movie.

The optician went up to him and spoke sternly, 'Excuse me, aren't you the man whose eyesight is so bad you can't fight for your country?'

The spiv looked up and said quickly, 'Ah, there you are, conductor. Can you tell me, does this bus go straight to Marble Arch?'

August 21st

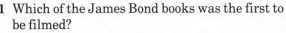

Bathroom Brain-teasers

1 Which of the James Bond books was the first to be filmed?
2 How much will you give me for Cleo Rocos' home telephone number?
3 Can you name all four Monkees?
4 Can you name all the kings of England since 973?
5 Spanish scientists have found a way to increase production of milk – what is it?

(Answers at foot of next page)

Many Happy Returns of the day to Princess Margaret (1930) and movie-buff Barry Norman (1933).

August 22nd

One of the great wits of all time was born today in 1893, so hats off and **Happy Birthday** to Dorothy Parker, famed for such bons mots as:

'The two most beautiful words in the English language are "cheque enclosed".'

In 1927 she wrote the following bitter-sweet poem, called *Resumé:*

> Razors pain you;
> Rivers are damp;
> Acids stain you;
> And drugs cause cramp;
> Guns aren't lawful;
> Nooses give;
> Gas smells awful;
> You might as well live.

August 23rd

Make a list of things which drive you bananas with frustration, and I'll bet bureaucrats come somewhere near the top – especially when you have to fill in one of those forms to claim insurance. Mind you, it must be fun being the person who gets to read the claims, especially when you receive excuses like these (all genuine) from motorists involved in prangs:

'A pedestrian hit me and went under the car . . .'

'While pulling away from the kerb I glanced at my mother-in-law and drove into the river . . .'

And there was the recent case of the motorist whose windscreen was smashed by a large owl. The insurance company asked, 'What, in your opinion, caused the accident? The claimant responded, 'The owl forgot to hoot . . .'

Brain-teaser Answers

1) *Dr No.* 2) Only on days with a 'Y' in them. 3) Davy Jones, Peter Tork, Mike Nesmith, Mickey Dolenz. 4) Neither can I. 5) They've given their cows false teeth so they can chew and digest grass more easily.

August 24th

Astro-loogical personality profile for all those born under the sign of

♑ ♒ **VIRGO** ♍ ♈

(August 24th – September 23rd): Notoriously duplicitous, mean-spirited and lazy when it comes to changing sheets, you should remember to think twice before falling in love with a Virgoan. Other things to remember include: *a)* cancelling the milk before you go on holiday; *b)* never taking anything said by an estate agent at face value; *c)* avoiding the urge to break wind in front of members of the Royal Family.

August 25th

THE
KENNY EVERETT
GUIDE TO SURVIVAL IN THE
TWENTIETH CENTURY

In the interests of maintaining friendships, never go to a dinner party with a dead fish stapled to your ear-lobes.

Other things not to do at dinner parties include:

a) Taking pot-shots at your host's children with an air-rifle.
b) Monopolising the conversation with details of your appendix operation.
c) Producing what's left of your appendix in a glass bottle and passing it round for all to see.

Happy Birthday to Sean Connery, the original James Bond – born on this day in 1930. Did you know that author of the 007 books, Ian Fleming, wanted Cary Grant to play the part of James Bond?

August 26th

Julius Caesar's first invasion of Britain began on this day in 55BC. (Let me just correct one popular misquotation normally ascribed to old Julius. Shakespeare's play was entirely misleading when it came to the bit about the conspirators. There *were* no conspirators. An eyewitness to the event has recently revealed that Brutus was a greedy old sod who regularly helped himself to more than his fair share of dumplings. On the fateful day, Caesar got extremely miffed and chastised Brutus, saying, 'Oi, ate two, Brute.' In the ensuing battle for the dumpling, Caesar was stabbed by a fondue fork and shuffled off this mortal coil.)

Pay close attention if you have a birthday some time this year, because here comes this week's **Astro-loogical forecast**.

SAGITTARIUS

A major revelation is on the way this week when you discover the Meaning of Life! Unfortunately, you will leave it in the back pocket of your jeans and it will be chewed up in the wash. Affairs of the heart are to the fore this week; also affairs of the liver, kidneys and inner thigh.

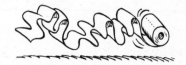

August 27th

Happy Birthday to Chinese philosopher Confucius (551–479 BC), among whose many sayings were, 'have no friends not equal to yourself'; 'study the past if you would divine the future'; and 'be nice to your neighbours, especially if you drive over their cat'. What a mind!

Happy Birthday also to the legendary Samuel Goldwyn (1882–1974) who is fondly remembered for the great goofs (or should that be 'gooves'?) he made, like:

'Anyone who goes to a psychiatrist ought to have his head examined.'

'An oral contract is not worth the paper it's written on.'

'In two words – impossible.'

August 28th

Bathroom Brain-teasers

1 Who directed *Ghandi, Cry Freedom* and *Oh, What a Lovely War?* (To give you a clue, he's celebrating his birthday today.)
2 Who played Alf Garnett's 'silly old moo'?
3 What does M.A.S.H. stand for?
4 What is frost?
5 How many times its own weight can an ant pull?

(Answers at foot of page)

August 29th

Happy Birthday to Sir Dickie-Pooh Attenborough (1923), director of *Ghandi, Cry Freedom* and *Oh, What A Lovely War*. And many happy returns to Lenny Henry (1958).

Today's Loo Laff

A young, newly-married man went to the pub for a night out with the lads. The subject turned to sex, and the man spent most of the evening regaling his mates with details of his exploits. When he returned home late, his wife asked what had kept him so long.

'We were talking,' he said.

'About what?'

'Oh . . . er . . . sailing.'

Brain-teaser Answers

1) Sir Richard Attenborough. 2) Dandy Nichols. 3) Mobile Army Surgical Hospital. 4) Frozen dew. 5) Ten.

The following day the man's wife bumped into one of the pub mates in the local supermarket. Her husband's friend winked a lot, telling her how much he'd enjoyed her husband's stories the night before. 'You're very lucky to be married to such an expert,' he said.

The woman frowned. 'That's odd,' she said. 'He's only done it twice. The first time he was sick. The second time his hat blew off.'

August 30th

Many Happy Returns to Denis 'Silly Billy' Healey (1917), who livened up British politics for many years. Once, when he was attacked over his budget proposals by Sir Geoffrey Howe, he remarked that it was, 'rather like being savaged by a dead sheep'.

Most politicians, it seems to me, are slightly potty, but I quite like potty people. Especially astronomer Patrick Moore, who has a fiendishly clever way of dealing with the even pottier people who write him daft letters. He takes the letter from Correspondent A, scribbles on it, 'this seems to echo your note – please respond', and then sends if off to Correspondent B. The two fruit-cakes then begin a long and happy pen-pal relationship, leaving Potty Patrick free to spend time pottering around with the telescope. Brilliant!

August 31st

And speaking of fruit-cakes **Happy Birthday** to the grand-daddy of them all, Caligula, the Roman Emperor who not only declared himself a god, but went on to appoint his horse to the senate!

Newsflash from the Department of Fascinating Facts . . . !

Did you know that the most popular name in the UK is Smith (nearly three-quarters of a million) . . . ? Of course you did. But take a guess at the *fifth* most popular name in the country. The answer is Patel.

And if the Smiths, Browns, Jones, Johnsons and Patels think *they've* got problems, spare a thought for China which has no fewer than 75 million people called Chan!

September 1st

THE KENNY EVERETT GUIDE TO SURVIVAL IN THE TWENTIETH CENTURY

Never invade Poland on an empty stomach. (Adolf Hitler invaded Poland on this day in 1939, and look what happened to him!)

Do you know how many words there are in the English language? And do you know how few of those words most of us use in everyday conversation?

Neither do I.

But it's never too late to expand your vocabulary. See if you can use these words in a sentence:

1 Kedogenous.
2 Judicious.
3 Defenestration.

1 This is a condition which arises from worry, i.e. 'May I borrow your hair? I'm suffering from kedogenous alopecia.' (That should shut 'em up!)
2 As in, 'hands that judicious can feel soft as your face . . .'
3 Throwing something (or someone) out of a window, i.e. 'I'm so sorry, Mr Everett can't come to the telephone to discuss his tax demand. He's busy defenestrating.'

September 2nd

Once again it's time to peek into the forwardsness of time and find out what fate has in store. This week's **Astroloogical Forecast** is for

 CANCER

Career matters are in for a major boost this week when you are invited to head a Government Enquiry into Joan Collins's cleavage. Now that you've discovered the sordid details of your other half's infidelity, you must start to pick up the pieces of your shattered life. (If you *haven't* discovered the details of your other half's affair, I do hope I haven't spoiled anything for you.)

September 3rd

Bathroom Brain-teasers

1 Where was the Marble Arch originally intended for?
2 Who were The Joker, The Riddler and The Penguin?
3 If you have blue eyes, what will happen to them as you get older?
4 On average, how long does a coin stay in circulation?
5 What do you get if you cross a parrot with a homing pigeon?

(Answers at foot of page)

Many Happy Returns of the day to Raquel Welch (1940).

September 4th

Today's Loo Laff

An Indian Chief was asked by a young brave how all the members of the tribe came to have such romantic names.

'Well, I always decide the names of my people,' said the Chief. 'And I base my decision on the first thing I see after the child is

---

Brain-teaser Answers

1) As a gateway to Buckingham Palace, but the arch was too narrow to accommodate the wheels of the Royal carriages, so it was moved to its present site. 2) Batman's adversaries. 3) They will get lighter. 4) Twenty-five years. 5) A bird that can ask its own way home if it gets lost.

born. Over there is your cousin, Passing Clouds – named after the clouds I saw just after he first saw light of day. And over there is Running Deer – so called because, as I left the maternity wigwam after he was born, I saw a pair of deer running through the woods.

'But tell me, Two Dogs Bonking, why do you ask this question?'

September 5th

Happy Birthday to Freddie Mercury (1946) and American comedian Bob Newhart (1929). As far as I'm concerned, Newhart's well and truly earned his place in heaven thanks to classic comedy routines like 'The Discovery Of Tobacco' and 'The Driving Instructor'. Do you remember that wonderful monologue he does with a female pupil . . . ?

' . . . er, how fast were you going when Mr Adams jumped from the car? . . . Seventy-five? . . . And where was that? . . . In your driveway? . . . How far had Mr Adams gotten in the lesson? . . . Backing out? . . .

September 6th

Happy Birthday to former good-time-girl turned happily-married mum, Britt Ekland (1942). In her days as a naughty sex-pot sirenipoo, she once remarked, 'I say I don't sleep with married men, but what I mean is that I don't sleep with *happily* married men.'

Entirely unconnected with Britt's birthday is a Bette Davis scorching put-down about a woman famed for enjoying the company of men: 'She was the original good time had by all.'

September 7th

Happy Birthday to Queen Elizabeth I (1533–1603) whose most famous saying is, 'I know I have the body of a weak and feeble woman, but I have the heart and stomach, liver and onions of a King, and of a King of England too.'

One of her descendants, Prince Edward, recently signed on as a production assistant with Andrew Lloyd Webber's production company. Our Royal Mole reveals that, with his new contacts, Lloyd Webber is working on a follow-up to *Cats* – it'll be called *Corgis*. Princess Margaret is to star in a new musical about a cocktail-drinking Argentinian; the title song, *Don't Cry For Me, Margharita,* will be released shortly. And the Princess Royal is believed to be considering a role in another Andrew Lloyd Webber production: *Princess Anne and Her Amazing Technicolour Horse Blanket.*

September 8th

Many Happy Returns of the day to the man with the most infectious laugh in show-biz, Sir Harry Secombe (1921).

PERSONALITY POSERS:
Yes, time to squirm and test your scruples again as I present another batch of character-testing questions.
1 You find a wallet in the street containing £10,000 in cash. Do you *a*) hand it in to the police? *b*) Take over Stringfellow's and invite all your friends to the party of the year?
   (If you answer *a*, well done. If you answer *b*, can I come?)
2 At a tea-party given by your wealthy aunt, you accidentally pour a bottle of cyanide into her cup of Typhoo. Your aunt dies a horrible, lingering death in front of your very eyes. Do you *a*) say you're very, very, *very* sorry indeed and promise never to do it again? or *b*) offer to make a fresh pot of tea?

September 9th

Hello, star-gazers! Here comes this week's chance to see what the Zodiac's up to, and today's forecast is for

♐ ♑ GEMINI ♓ ♊

At last all your carefully-laid plans will come to fruition and you will finally achieve your lifelong ambition to become a Nolan Sister. You share your birth sign with Robert Redford, and he's asked me to remind you to return it when you've finished.

DAFT DEFINITIONS:
'A critic is a man who knows the way but cannot drive the car.' (Kenneth Tynan)

Personally, I won't hear a word against critics, although I agree with the person who said that 'asking a writer how he feels about critics is like asking a lamp-post how it feels about dogs'.

September 10th

Nothing of any historical importance happened on this day at all. *Ever.* It's the most boring day of the year; the sort of day when you'll do anything for a laugh – even pop in to see your local taxidermist and tell him to get stuffed.

A cat-loving friend of mine recently took her two dead cats to be stuffed.

'Do you want them mounted, Madam?' asked the stiff-stuffer.

'No, thanks,' she replied, 'just holding hands.'

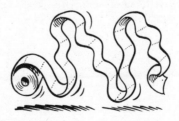

September 11th

Bathroom Brain-teasers

1 Which country once issued a postage stamp in recognition of the world's heaviest smoker?
2 How did Yul Brynner 'come back from the dead'?
3 Whose song, 'I Want Your Sex', was banned by the BBC?
4 What is a cat's favourite TV show?
5 What is the proper name of the bit of the body we call the funny bone?

(Answers at foot of page)

Happy Birthday to D.H. Lawrence, who was born on this day in 1885 and died in 1930. Most famous as the author of *Lady Chatterley's Lover,* few people know that Lawrence wrote a number of sequels to this classic book.

The series follows Lady Chatterley's life and includes *Lady Chatterley's Husband, Lady Chatterley's Bit on the Side, Lady Chatterley's Husband Catches Her with her Bit on the Side and gets a bit Cross, Lady Chatterley's Divorce Lawyer,* ending up with *Lady Chatterley Marries her Divorce Lawyer but Carries on Seeing her Ex-husband on the Quiet on the Condition that the Gamekeeper can keep his Job.*

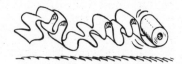

Brain-teaser Answers
1) Albania. 2) He recorded a series of TV commercials before his death from lung cancer to warn people of the perils of smoking. 3) George Michael. 4) Miami Mice. 5) The humerus.

September 12th

Today's Loo Laff

The scene: the Pearly Gates. St Peter is welcoming three new arrivals and he asks the first man what had caused his death.

'I came home early and found a man in bed with my wife. He jumped out of the window and tried to run down the fire-escape. So I threw the fridge out of the window, trying to hit him. The strain must have caused a massive heart attack.'

St Peter asked the second man what had caused his death.

'A blow from a heavy falling object.'

St Peter then turned to a third man. 'And how did you come to pop your clogs, sir?'

'Well, I'm not really too sure,' said the man. 'There I was sitting in this fridge . . .'

September 13th

PHILOSOPHICAL STATEMENT OF THE DAY

'Where there's a will, there's a relative.'

A friend of mine recently made his will. He's a great believer in reincarnation, so he simply left everything to himself.

I like the story of the philandering millionaire who wanted to leave his fortune to the woman who had been his 'personal assistant' for twenty years, but didn't want to be too obvious. His Last Will and Testicles finished with the words ' . . . and so, to my beloved cat, Piddles, I leave my entire fortune. And to my loyal personal assistant, Miss Dingleberry, I leave my cat.'

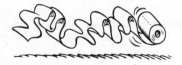

September 14th

Dear Uncle Ken...

I am at my wits' end and I don't know where to turn. As a lonely spinster, I always relied for company on my cat – Vindaloo. Recently she's gone missing. The man from the Social Services said I should place an ad. in the paper, but I know it wouldn't do any good because she can't read. Above all, I miss Vindaloo because she was the best chess partner I ever had. (The man from the Social Services was very impressed when I told him I had a cat that played chess. I told him Vindaloo wasn't *that* smart: last time we played, I beat her four games to three.) My question is this: how can I be sure the little light goes off when I shut the fridge door?

Uncle Ken writes:

There are many mysteries in life: the greatest of these is the one about the light in the fridge. Thank you for bringing it to my attention. It's ready for collection any time you want it back.

September 15th

Happy Birthday to mystery writer Agatha Christie (1890–1976).

Here are two things NOT achieved by Agatha Christie:

She never balanced seven golf balls on top of one another: that distinction went to Lang Martin of North Carolina.

And as far as we know, she didn't guzzle her way through 96 sausages in 6 minutes. (The banger-nosher in question – who ate one *every four seconds*! – was New Yorker Steve Meltzer.)

September 16th

Just imagine all those planetary bodies, stars, satellites and heavenly aspects whizzing about up there, all in order that I can bring you this week's **Astro-loogical Forecast.** This week, it's the turn of

♈ ♓ ♌ **LEO** ♉ ♊ ♋

It's time to stop making mountains out of molehills. Instead, try making a Mother's Day card out of three lamb chops. If things have been a little on the dull side recently, try fondling the private parts of complete strangers – you'll find things will soon liven up.

Happy Birthday to Russ Abbott (1947) and Lauren 'Betty' Bacall (1924).

September 17th

Many Happy Returns of the day to Mrs Mel Brooks (actress Anne Bancroft), born on this day in 1931.

Can you imagine spending your life with Mel Brooks? I wonder if he starts each day with one of his philosophical comedy routines, like this excerpt from a recent interview in *The Guardian*:

'Between projects I go into the park and bite the grass and wail, "Why do You make me aware of the fact that I have to die one day?" God says, "Please, I have Chinese people yelling at me, I haven't time for this." I say all right. God is like a Jewish waiter, he has too many tables.'

September 18th

Happy Birthday to Greta Garbo (1905) who was recently spotted in New York's Central Park, plaiting her hair with blades of grass. When a passing policeman asked what she was up to, she replied, 'I vant to be a lawn . . .'

If you need an excuse to have a party today, you could always celebrate the feast day of the Patron Saint of air travellers and pilots, Saint Joseph of Cupertino. Old Joe is remembered chiefly as the world's first levitating Saint.

September 19th

Bathroom Brain-teasers

1 What are the ten most commonly used letters of the alphabet?
2 What time does the clock printed above the leading article in *The Times* always show?
3 What were T.S. Eliot's christian names?
4 At what speed does a wind become a hurricane?
5 Can you name all the people who survived the *Titanic* disaster?

(Answers at foot of page)

Happy Birthday to Twiggy who was born today in (1949). Quick! What is Twiggy's real name? Answer: Lesley Hornby.

---

brain-teaser Answers

1) E, T, A, O, I, N, S, H, R, D. 2) 4.30 3) Thomas Stearns. 4) 73 miles per hour. 5) Neither can I.

September 20th

Happy Birthday to one of the great beauties of the world (nearly as beautiful as my knees), Sophia Loren (1934).

Today's Loo Laff

A beautiful young woman sitting in the corner of a railway carriage kept tearing bits out of her newspaper, folding them in half, screwing them up and hurling them out of the window.

Anxious to find an opening conversational gambit, a young man asked why she was doing it.

'To keep the elephants away.'

'But there aren't any elephants,' said the young man.

'No,' smiled the girl. 'It's very effective, isn't it?'

September 21st

Best-selling author and 'superwoman' Shirley Conran was born on this day in 1932 and earned the undying gratitude of harassed housewives all over the world when she declared: 'Life is too short to stuff a mushroom.'

And **Happy Birthday** to Larry 'JR' Hagman (1931). A bit of an eccentric, Larry apparently refuses to utter a single word on Sundays. He says he needs to re-charge his batteries and prepare for the week ahead.

September 22nd

Many Happy Returns of the day to Princess Anne's hubbie-poo, Captain Mark Phillips (1948).

Can you remember

a) Which former Liberal MP used to advertise dog food?

b) For which booze ad. did Leonard Rossiter team up with Joan Collins?

c) Which petrol company claimed to 'Put a Tiger In Your Tank'?

ANSWERS: a) Clement Freud. b) Cinzano. c) Esso.

September 23rd

The Zodiac's in a bit of a turmoil this week, star-lovers. Mars is due to enter the Milky Way, but is being thwarted by Picnic, Marathon and a packet of wine-gums. Thankfully I was able to do the astro-chart for all those born under the sign of

♏ SGORPIO ♐

A friend's practical joke will backfire on you this week. You will discover that your knees have been stapled together, and your nipples have been offered as a sacrifice to the Aztec god of microwave cooking.

Happy Birthday to Mickey 'Let's Do The Show Right Here' Rooney (1920) and Bruce 'Born to Run' Springsteen (1949).

September 24th

Happy Birthday to Linda McCartney (1941). Poor girl, when she married Paul she had to put up with all sorts of nasty insults from his heartbroken fans, like:

'What do you call a dog with wings?'

'Linda McCartney.'

Never mind Linda, cheer yourself up with the **Astro-loogical personality profile** for all those born under the sign of

♎ ♋ LIBRA ♌ ♍

(September 24th – October 23rd):

Suave, sophisticated, debonair . . . these are just three of the words most Librans know how to spell. Irresistibly attractive to members of the opposite sex, Librans are well-known for breaking hearts. (They often break other things as well, like window-panes and tea-cups.)

Famous Librans: Margaret Thatcher; Roger Moore; Brigitte Bardot. Completely unknown Librans: Alice Spong of Margate; Dave's Mum.

September 25th

Happy Birthday to the lovely Ronnie 'Master of the *double-entendre*' Barker (1919), who recently decided to retire from the world of television. He's opened up an antiques shop, no doubt specialising in large chests and highly polished knockers!

On this day in 1956 the first transatlantic telephone cable between Britain and America came into use.
  PHONE PHUN . . . (courtesy of Eric and Ernie)
  'Hey! Answer the phone! Answer the phone!'
  'But it's not ringing . . .'
  'Why leave everything to the last minute?'

September 26th

Happy Birthday to stylist and singer Bryan Ferry (1945).

HELPFUL HINTS DEPARTMENT
Q: What's the best way to decide whether you should use a nail or a screw when doing some D-I-Y around the house?
A: Bang in a nail. If the wood splits, you should have used a screw.

Q: How do you make sure your wall paper hangs properly?
A: Try to avoid getting in between the wall and the paper. A human being trapped in this position will leave unsightly bulges, thus making a smooth finish impossible.

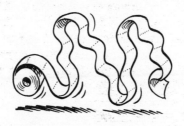

September 27th

Bathroom Brain-teasers

1 Who wrote *Lady Chatterley's Lover*? Was it *a*) D. H. Lawrence or *b*) D. H. Evans.
2 What is the FBI's motto?
3 What is comedian Steve Martin's motto?
4 What is unusual about the Mona Lisa's face?
5 Why do barristers wear black?

(Answers at foot of page)

Happy Birthday to Olivia 'Squeaky-Clean' Newton-John (1948):

September 28th

Bon anniversaire to sex-kitten-turned-animal-fanatic Brigitte Bardot (1934).

Today's Loo Laff

After a good night out, the drunken old soak staggered out of the pub and nearly fell over a fitness-freak who was doing press-ups on the pavement outside.

The drunk swayed unsteadily on his feet and stared at the

Brain-teaser Answers

1) Either *a* or *b* 2) Fidelity, Bravery, Integrity. 3) Never do your best stuff. 4) She has no eyebrows. 5) Because they are supposed to be still in mourning for Queen Mary who died in 1694. (Daft if you ask me: most of them didn't even send flowers to the funeral.)

energetic man's activities for a full ten minutes. Finally, he spoke.

'Excushe me, young . . . hic . . . man . . . I think you should know that someone's stolen your girlfriend.'

September 29th

On this day in 490 BC the Persians bashed the living daylights out of the Greeks at the Battle of Marathon. This was followed a year later by the Battle of Milky Way, when the Greeks retaliated by coating the hated Persians in a mixture of chewy caramel and milk chocolate. Exactly one year later, the Persian gods got their revenge by showing Athens with a plague of Rowntree's Fruit Pastilles. Isn't history fascinating . . . ?

September 30th

Hello, star-gazers everywhere. This week's forecast is for

♐ ♑ **GEMINI** ♓ ♊

A family row may be brewing and you will be required to take a firm stand – but don't forget to put it back when you've finished. People born under this sign are generally known for their sensitivity, charm and dazzling good looks. You, however, are the exception to the rule and are renowned for your enormous nose and horrendously smelly feet.

Happy Birthday to American writer Truman Capote (1924–1984) who dismissed a rival's work by saying, 'that's not writing, that's typing'.

October 1st

Happy Birthday to Julie Andrews (1935), Walter Matthau (1920) and Jimmy Carter (1924).

Did you know that even when a President has retired, he is still supposed to be addressed as 'Mr President' for the rest of his life?

On this day in 1908 Henry Ford introduced the famous Model T car, priced at $850. Ford was a crafty old devil and there's a famous story about a manufacturer who wrote to him asking for the highly lucrative contract to supply all the nuts and bolts for the first mass-produced automobile. Ford insisted that the nuts and bolts should be packed in wooden cases, and gave exact specifications as to the strength, width, length and construction of the cases. When the cases arrived at the factory by the thousand, Ford ordered them to be unpacked and put to one side. The clever swine had saved a fortune by getting the nuts and bolts factory to supply the basic frame for the car, absolutely free!

October 2nd

Happy Birthday to Groucho Marx (1890–1977). Let's celebrate with a few of his best quips:

'I never forget a face, but in your case I'll make an exception.'

'Many years ago I chased a woman for almost two years, only to discover her tastes were exactly like mine: we were both crazy about girls.'

'No one is completely unhappy at the failure of his best friend.'

October 3rd

THE
KENNY EVERETT
GUIDE TO SURVIVAL IN THE
TWENTIETH CENTURY

When confronted by a bull in a field, don't stop to ask him if he's colour blind unless *a*) you don't mind missing your bus; or *b*) you don't need both your arms.

Bathroom Brain-teasers

1 What was Quentin Crisp's attitude to housework?
2 Which animal has to go through the longest pregnancy?
3 When the escalator was first introduced onto the London Underground System, how did London Transport persuade people that it was safe to use?
4 Who was Playboy's first centrefold?
5 Bulls are colour blind – true or false?

(Answers at foot of page)

October 4th

Happy Birthday to silent movie-star, Buster Keaton (1895–1966). Among his most famous lines were '. . . . . ! . . . .' and '. . . . . !!*!'

And on this day in 1970, rock singer Janis Joplin went to the Great Juke Box in the Sky. She was a hard-drinking, dope-taking woman who definitely lived life in the fast lane. Her will contained a bequest of $2,500, 'so that my friends can get blasted after I'm gone . . .'

Brain-teaser Answers

1) 'Never bother with it: after the first four years, you don't notice the dust.' 2) An elephant – 645 days! 3) They hired a man with a wooden leg to travel up and down all day long, demonstrating the escalator's efficiency and safety. 4) Marilyn Monroe. 5) True. (In which case, why bother with all that red cape stuff . . . ?)

October 5th

Today's Loo Laff

The solicitor was becoming suspicious about one of his new clients, a wealthy widow who had outlived three husbands. When her fourth husband died, he attended the reading of the will and discovered that she was the sole beneficiary.

After the formalities had been dispensed with, the solicitor asked her what had caused the deaths of her husbands.

'Oh, the first one died from eating poisoned mushrooms.'

'And the second?'

'He died from eating poisoned mushrooms.'

'And the third?'

'Poisoned mushrooms.'

'And the fourth?'

'He wouldn't eat his mushrooms.'

October 6th

FOOD FOR THOUGHT:

Next time you're invited to a Bedouin wedding feast, watch what they serve with the sherry. A favourite snack at Bedouin bashes is roast camel. If you'd like to try the dish in the privacy of your own home, here's the recipe:

Take one camel.

Boil one dozen eggs.

Stuff the boiled eggs into a dozen fish (preferably dead ones).

Stuff the egg-filled fish into twelve chickens.

Stuff the egg and fish-filled chickens into a roast sheep.

Stuff the egg, fish, chicken-filled sheep into the camel.

Place in a pre-heated oven at 350 degrees and baste regularly.

Finally, leave the camel right where it is and go out for a pizza.

October 7th

Happy Birthday to a man they call The Abominable Abo – Clive James (whose real first name is Vivien), born today in 1939.

I've been casting my tarot, consulting my crystal ball, gazing at my tea-leaves and drying my socks – all in order to be able to bring you this week's **Astro-loogical Forecast** and it's for all those born under the sign of:

♈ ♒ **RABIES** ♓ ♍ ♑

A bad week for breaking promises, but a good week for breaking wind. A stroke of luck is likely tomorrow when you discover a cure for the common cold which can also be used as an oven glove. Be prepared for a surprise nocturnal visit from a tribe of Pygmies.

October 8th

Former Argentinian President Juan Peron was born today in 1895, but there's not much point in sending him a birthday card: he snuffed it in 1974.

Funny how no one remembers him but his old lady, Eva Peron, lives on in everyone's memories – thanks to Tim Rice and Andrew Lloyd Webber's *Evita*.

HISTORY LESSON:
Funny what people used to do for fun in ye olde days. Did you know that it used to be the custom to pass a newly born child through the rind of a cheese? Not long after, someone invented television and the old custom began to die out.

October 9th

Happy Birthday to John Lennon, now sadly gone to the Great Strawberry Field In The Sky. He was really fab, gear and all that other Sixties stuff. I remember one day being invited for dinner at his house in Weybridge, Surrey. This was at the height of his famous-ness, when he was millionairing all over the place, so I didn't eat for days expecting a mountain of caviare and champagne and quails' eggs. When I got there, Yoko opened a tin of Heinz tomato soup!

October 10th

Happy Birthday to Nicholas Parsons (1928) and Harold Pinter (1930). Doing research for this book, I've been dazzled and amazed at the number of coincidences which arise on birthdays. It's uncanny, don't you think, that two such similar geniuses were born on the same day. That's proof enough for me that there is something to this astrology lark, so put that in your pipe and don't let it spoil the broth.

(Incidentally, when Pinter was asked what one of his incredibly obscure plays was about, he replied 'The weasel under the cocktail cabinet.' So now you know.)

October 11th

THE

KENNY EVERETT

GUIDE TO SURVIVAL IN THE

TWENTIETH CENTURY

Never pick up a telephone receiver with a mouthful of peanuts. It's much easier to use your hand.

Bathroom Brain-teasers

1 What does 'ludo' mean?
2 How do you pronounce the surnames 'Cholmondely' and 'Featherstonehaugh'?
3 Under what name did Simon and Garfunkel originally record?
4 Who were the stars of the disasterous film flop *Ishtar*?
5 How does a funambulist walk?

(Answers at foot of page)

October 12th

Many Happy Returns of the day to operatic tenor, Luciano Pavarotti (1935). I can't say I know much about opera, but I have a hunch a geezer called David Randolph may have been right when he said, *'Parsifal* is the kind of opera that starts at six o'clock. After it has been going three hours, you look at your watch and it says 6.20.'

Today's Loo Laff

Adam and Eve were in the Garden of Eden when the word came down from above that the time had come to name the animals.
'Right,' said Adam, 'that one over there, let's call it . . . a rhinoceros.'
'Why a rhinoceros?' asked Eve.
'Because it looks like one, stupid!'

Brain-teaser Answers

1) I play (in Latin). 2) Chumley and Fanshaw. (What a wacky world we live in!) 3) Tom and Jerry. 4) Warren Beatty and Dustin Hoffman. (It cost $42,000,000!) 5) Very carefully – a funambulist is a tightrope walker.

October 13th

Happy Birthday to Margaret Hilda Thatcher (1925). Whatever your politics, she's a remarkable woman. American Secretary of State George Schultz said, 'If I were married to her, I'd be sure to have dinner ready when she got home.'

Clive James described her as sounding 'like the Book Of Revelations read out over a railway station public address system by a headmistress of a certain age wearing calico knickers'.

And a man called Edward Pearce once observed, 'Margaret Thatcher will never speak well on television. Her impulse to tell the microphone to pull itself together is too strong.'

October 14th

Have you ever wondered what it would be like to see into the future? Well, now you can – thanks to Uncle Ken's **Astroloogical Forecasting** service, available in blue, yellow and all good record shops. Today's lucky Zodiac sign is

when you accidentally leave your nose on the bus. In times of doubt and despair, remember the words of the ancient philosopher Portcullis: ' . . . desperandum nil, West Bromwich Albion 3 . . .'

♉ ♊ **TAURUS** ♌ ♎

The absent-mindedness for which you are renowned will reach new heights this week

Many Happy Returns of the day to Roger Moore (1927) and the man they call the Peter Pan of Pop, Cliff Richard (1940).

October 15th

Uncle Ken's Agony Column

Dear Uncle Ken...

I am only nine years old, but already I feel as though the world is against me. I asked my Mum what I should be when I grow up, and she suggested I become a Lollipop Man . . . at Brands Hatch.

When I was three, my Dad taught me to swim by rowing me three miles out to sea and making me swim back to shore. The hardest part was getting out of the sack first. I have two questions:

a) What is the difference between elephants and fleas?
b) Do you believe in luck?

Uncle Ken writes:

a) An elephant can have fleas, but a flea can't have elephants.
b) Naturally: how else can we explain the success of people we don't like?

October 16th

Happy Birthday to Oscar Wilde (1854–1900). You could fill a cross-channel ferry with all the smart-alec remarks made by Old Oscar.

Oscar on families: 'Relations are simply a tedious pack of people who haven't the remotest knowledge of how to live, nor the smallest instinct about when to die.'

Oscar on hunting: 'The unspeakable in full pursuit of the uneatable.'

Oscar on alcohol: 'Work is the curse of the drinking classes.'

Oscar on his prison sentence: 'If this is the way Queen Victoria treats her prisoners, she doesn't deserve to have any.'

Oscar on falling over a roller-skate on the staircase: 'Who left that roller-skate there?'

October 17th

Bathroom Brain-teasers

1 How does a giraffe wash out its ears?
2 Name Steed's female sidekicks in *The Avengers*.
3 A tonsorialist is a posh name for what?
4 What does the word 'soviet' mean?
5 Name all seven of Snow White's dwarfs . . .

(Answers at foot of page)

Many Happy Returns of the day to gentle comedian, Kelly Monteith (1942).

Comedy's a funny business. Where do jokes come from? And what makes the comedians themselves laugh?

Groucho Marx had it about right:

'An amateur thinks it's funny if you dress a man up as an old lady, put him in a wheelchair and give the wheelchair a push that sends it spinning down a slope towards a wall. For a pro, it's got to be a *real* old lady . . .'

October 18th

Many Happy Returns of the day to Chuck Berry, who's been rockin' and rollin' since 1926.

PERSONALITY POSERS:
Test your moral courage again with these character condundrums (or should that be conundra . . . ?)

Brain-teaser Answers
1) With its tongue. (Go on, you try it.)　2) Honor Blackman, Diana Rigg, Linda Thorsen, Joanna Lumley.　3) A hairdresser.
4) Worker's council.　5) Dopey, Bashful, Sleepy, Grumpy, Doc, Happy and Sneezy.

1 A mega-rich person offers to marry you if you agree to eat a hundred slices of dandruff on toast. Do you *a*) run a mile, or *b*) run two miles?

2 Driving a fork-lift truck on your way to a bridge tournament, you accidentally run over a nun carrying an empty bottle of lemonade. Do you *a*) become annoyed at being late for the tournament, or *b*) take the lemonade bottle to the nearest off-licence and claim the deposit?

October 19th

The Russkies' version of Big Ben was cast on this day in 1773. It's the Kremlin's 20 foot-high 'King Of Bells', weighing over 200 tons. The only problem with this impressive piece of soviet know-how is that the King of Bells has never actually been rung; it got cracked as they were prising it from the mould. None of this comes as any surprise to Yours Truly. I went on a fact-finding jaunt to Russia recently, and among the facts I found:

a) Leningrad airport only has an outside loo.

b) Aeroflot planes are cleaned by a Russian peasant woman, using a broom.

c) And I can bring you the good news that the Russians are never, ever going to start World War Three. Judging by what I saw, they have enough trouble making a cup of tea.

October 20th

Feeling puny, unsuccessful, useless? Generally speaking, are you a complete waste of food? Well, here's something to make you feel even worse. Sir Richard Burton died on this day in 1890 (no, not Liz Taylor's jeweller – the other Richard Burton). Talk about over-achiever! He was a champion swordsman, an intrepid explorer and had a brain the size of a Christmas pudding: he wrote forty-three travel books and two volumes of poetry; translated sixteen volumes of *The Arabian Nights,* two volumes of Latin poetry and six volumes of Portugese literature, as well as books in Hindustani, Arabic and Sanskrit. And that was all before breakfast!

Today's Loo Laff

Did you hear about the flasher who went out looking for victims on a January night? It was so cold, he went up to women and described himself.

And while we're on the subject of sex . . .

Q: What's a Jewish blue film?

A: Ten minutes of sex, fifty minutes of guilt.

October 21st

Star time once again, loo-lovers, and this week it's the turn of

CAPRICORN

You need a break from routine – why not try licking the backs of your knees? While we're on the subject of Tupperware, the signs are that if you keep up your behaviour for much longer, you will shortly break the world record for promiscuity. You should be aware, however, the present world record is currently held by the person you are currently deceiving . . .

Happy Birthday to Alfred Nobel (1833–1896) and also to the tallest-ever Italian alcoholic, Hi Tiddley Eyetie.

October 22nd

PHILOSOPHICAL STATEMENT OF THE DAY

'There is nothing so peaceful as the sleep of the just. Except, perhaps, the sleep of the just-after.'

PERSONALITY POSERS:

1) While travelling on a bus you discover a diary filled with revealing and EXTREMELY NAUGHTY titbits about famous stars and politicians. Do you *a*) make a fortune by selling it to the *News of the World, or b*) make a fortune by selling it to the *Sunday People*?

October 23rd

Happy Birthday to US talk-show host Johnny Carson (1925) who opens every show with a comedy monologue. When Jimmy Carter was President he was dogged by his embarrassing brother, Billy; Carson quipped, 'Jimmy needs Billy like Van Gogh needs stereo.' He also has this important piece of medical advice: 'If you want to clear your system out, sit on a piece of cheese and swallow a mouse.'

October 24th

Astro-loogical personality profile for all those born under the sign of

♏ SCORPIO ♐

(October 24th – November 22nd):

Scorpio-born people tend to have masses of courage, energy and under-arm hair. Not renowned for their sense of humour, they find it hard to understand jokes. This is the favourite joke of everyone born under the sign of Scorpio:

Q: What did Tarzan say when he saw the elephants coming?

A: Here come the elephants.

Many Happy Returns of the day to crusty inquisitor, Sir Robin Day (1923).

October 25th

Happy Birthday to a whole host of geniuses (genuis–i ?), including Johann 'Blue Danube' Strauss (1825–1899), Georges 'Carmen' Bizet (1838–1875) and Pablo 'lots of squiggly lines on bits of canvas' Picasso (1881–1973).

Old Pablo was worth a bob or two when he popped his clogs, but he was just a beginner compared with the Sultan of Brunei, who has an annual income of $2,700 million! And if that's enough to make you throw away your piggy-bank, imagine being Frederick Smith, chairman of an American company whose 1982 income was $51,544,000 – $25,000 an hour:

October 26th

Bathroom Brain-teasers

1 What does a somnambulist do?
2 When was flogging abolished in Britain?
3 How many times does the letter 'z' occur in the word antelope?
4 What was David Niven's autobiography called?
5 What was Kenny Everett's autobiography called?

(Answers at foot of page)

Brain-teaser Answers

1) Sleep-walk. 2) Only recently: 1948. 3) It's about time you worked these things out for yourself. 4) *The Moon's A Balloon.* 5) *The Custard Stops At Hatfield.*

October 27th

Many Happy Returns of the day to one of the funniest men alive, John Cleese (1939). And happy birthday to Welsh poet Dylan Thomas who had a wicked sense of fun. His play *Under Milk Wood* was originally written for radio, and played a little joke on the dusty old fogies at the BBC by setting the action in the Welsh village of *Llareggub* which, spelt backwards is . . . (work it out for yourself!).

October 28th

Once again, we gaze heavenwards and take a peek-preview at what the fates have in store. This week's **Astro-loogical Forecast** is for

⫛♋ PISGES ♏ ♐

A stroke of luck if you're hunting for bargains this week – the signs are that you'll be able to pick up a very reasonably-priced pair of eighteenth-century nostrils.

DAFT DEFINITIONS:
Wedding: a necessary formality before securing a divorce.

October 29th

Today's Loo Laff

Lorraine: Will you remember me in a week's time?
Kevin: Yes, of course, darling.
Lorraine: Will you remember me in a month's time?
Kevin: What a silly question. Of *course* I will.
Lorraine: Will you remember me in a year's time?
Kevin: Yes, darling. I promise.
Lorraine: Knock knock.
Kevin: Who's there?
Lorraine: See, you've forgotten me already!

EXTREMELY IRRITATING QUESTION
Q: When using a typewriter, which ten-letter word can you type by just using the top row of the keyboard? (NB – there's a clue in the question.)
A: TYPEWRITER.

October 30th

Media Madness:
It was on this day in 1938 that Orson Welles produced a radio version of H. G. Wells's *The War Of The Worlds*. The broadcast followed a fictional Martian invasion of Earth, and was so realistic that millions of people all over America went beserk, convinced that they were being taken over by little green men. (A similar panic gripped the United States many years later when millions of Yanks fell for a TV sketch in which Ronald Reagan joked about becoming President. To this day, there are many Americans who still believe he is.)

Happy Birthday to film director Michael Winner (1935). Famous for being a tough cookie, he once said, 'Film-making is a team effort. My idea of a team effort is sixty people doing exactly what I tell them.'

October 31st

Happy Birthday to Jimmy "Owzaboutthatthenguysandgals' Savile (1926). And on the same day escapologist Harry Houdini – who had survived being tied up, shackled, chained, locked in an underwater 'coffin' and numerous other daredevil daftitudes – finally snuffed it. One of Houdini's boasts was that he could withstand being punched in the stomach. Amateur boxer Joselyn Whitehead decided to see if the boast was true – it wasn't.

THOUGHT FOR THE DAY
'Contraceptives should be used on every conceivable occasion.'
(Spike Milligan)

November 1st

TALL TALE
Spare a thought today for poor old Robert Wadlow, the tallest man ever to live. At the age of eight he was half an inch taller than his 5 feet 11 inches father. When he died he towered over everyone from an amazing 8 feet 11 inches – and was still growing.

Can you imagine the complications if he'd fallen for Pauline Musters – the world's shortest woman – who was just over 23 inches tall by the age of nineteen.

November 2nd

On this day in 1947 billionaire Howard Hughes made the maiden flight in his pet plane 'The Spruce Goose', which had the largest wingspan of any aircraft – 319 feet, 11 inches. The plane cost $40,000,000 dollars to develop and, after its first flight, languished in a hangar.

A real ladies' man, Hughes bought the massive RKO movie studio just in order to impress Ingrid Bergman. And, according to one Hollywood legend, he celebrated New Year's Eve in 1953 by hiring three suites in the Beverly Hills Hotel and installing a different woman in each room.

But I'm not too sure how much of a romantic Hughes was. Apparently he used to call Veronica Lake at five o'clock in the morning – not to whisper sweet nothings, but to ask her to drive him to the airport.

November 3rd

Happy Birthday to lovely Lulu (1948). Did you know her real name is Marie Lawrie? Or that when she recorded her first hit 'Shout' she had a heavy cold. Next time you hear it on the radio, listen closely and see if you can hear a tiny sneeze during the second chorus.

Bathroom Brain-teasers

1 Why did the skinhead cross the road?
2 What is the only fish which can hold an object in its tail?
3 What do you call someone who is afraid of colours?
4 What do you call someone who is afraid of cream cheese?
5 Who is the world's most irritating person?

(Answers at foot of page)

November 4th

If you're feeling miserable, depressed, lonely, forlorn, unloved, unwanted and generally down-in-the-dumps, here's some helpful advice – pull yourself together. And cheer yourself up with this week's Zodiac forecast, especially if you're born under the sign of

♑ ♒ **VIRGO** ♍ ♈

A good-looking stranger will enter your life and will help you to find peace, harmony and the remote-control for the television. A stroke of luck is in store this week when you discover a document which makes you the rightful owner of Mikhail Gorbachev's bald spot.

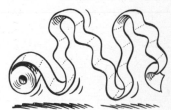

November 5th

Many Happy Returns of the day to Art 'Bright Eyes' Garfunkel (1941). And **Happy Birthday** to the famous plot to blow up the Houses of Parliament which took place on November 5th 1605. According to some people, Guy Fawkes was the only sensible person ever to enter the House of Commons.

Today's Loo Laff

A man found an anteater on the bus. He asked the conductor what he should do with it.

'I'd take it to the zoo if I were you,' said the conductor.

The next day the man got on the bus, followed by the anteater on a lead.

'I thought you were going to take it to the zoo,' said the conductor.

'That's right,' replied the man. 'I took him to the zoo yesterday. Today I'm taking him to the cinema.'

November 6th

PERSONALITY POSERS:

1 If you were stranded on a desert island and could choose your companion, would it be *a*) someone very sexy, or *b*) someone very intelligent? (Personally, I'd like to be stranded with someone who knows how to build a raft.)

2 A friend offers you £10,000 to shave off your hair. Part of the deal is that you mustn't ever discuss your reason for doing so. What do you do?

November 7th

Happy Birthday to evangelist Billy Graham (1918) who seems to have a lot of intriguingly precise information about Him Upstairs. Billy once claimed that Heaven is 1,600 miles above the Earth.

On this day in 1783, the last public hanging in Britain took place at Tyburn, which is now the site of Marble Arch. I'm totally against capital punishment myself, except for really serious crimes like plumbers who promise to show up at 9.00 a.m. and don't appear until the following Tuesday WHEN THEY LEAVE A NOTE SAYING, 'we called to unblock your pipes, but you were out.' AAARGH!!! Other criminals who should be punished by death (at least) include people who double-park by your car and block you in; and also people who insist on telling you in painstaking detail about the problems they're having with their builders.

November 8th

What a lovely day for rushing out into the street with no clothes on and shouting 'Happy Birthday' to Ken "Diddyman" Dodd, born on this day in 1927.

THE
KENNY EVERETT
GUIDE TO SURVIVAL IN THE
TWENTIETH CENTURY

Never invest every penny you possess in an ardvaark-pickling venture.

November 9th

Happy Birthday to the indomitable Katharine Hepburn (1909), who doesn't seem to have a very high opinion of her profession: 'Acting is the most minor of gifts and not a very high-class way of earning a living. After all, Shirley Temple could do it at the age of four.'

And while we're on the subject, Glenda Jackson once said: 'The important thing in acting is to be able to laugh and cry. If I have to cry, I think of my sex life. If I have to laugh, I think of my sex life.'

November 10th

Happy Birthday to Tim Rice (1944). And on this day in 1871 Sir Henry Stanley made headline news when he tracked down Dr Livingstone on the shores of Lake Tanganyika.

Other headline stories which have passed into legend include the story about a mental patient who assaulted two launderette attendants before escaping: *Nut Screws Washers and Bolts*; and the report in the *Gateshead Post* which announced details of a local crime: *Chip Shop Owner Battered Man*. But my favourite headline comes from *Private Eye*'s story about a librarian's strike in Essex. The item was headed: *Book Lack In Ongar*.

November 11th

Many Happy Returns of the day to a great British Institution, comedienne and actress June Whitfield – born on this day in 1927.

This week's **Astro-loogical Forecast** is for

≈ AQUARIUS ♉

Good news is on the way soon. You will be invited to spend a long weekend in Denis Healey's eyebrows. There is a danger that you are being taken for granted by your workmates. One highly effective way to get noticed is to dress like Darth Vader and cover your colleagues with Greek yoghurt.

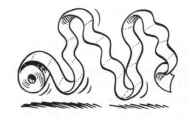

November 12th

Bathroom Brain-teasers

(special soap-opera section)

1 Which famous Coronation Street star was written out of the serial on Christmas Day, 1987?
2 Who played Angie in 'Eastenders'?
3 Which Beatle composed a version of the 'Crossroads' theme music?
4 Kate O'Mara's character in Dynasty rejoiced in which of the following fabulous names:
   a) Caress
   b) Fondle
   c) Zit.
5 Can you hum the theme music to Doctor Kildare?

(Answers at foot of page)

THOUGHT FOR THE DAY

A philosphical utterance supplied by music-hall star, Dan Leno:
   'Ah, what is man? Wherefore does he why? Whence did he whence? Whither is he withering? (My sentiments entirely . . .)

Brain-teaser Answers
1) Hilda Ogden. 2) Anita Dobson. 3) Paul McCartney. 4) Caress 5) Dee dum dee dee dee dum dum (etc. . .).

November 13th

Today's Loo Laff

Courtesy of Doctor Daft . . .
   'Doctor, Doctor, everyone thinks I'm going round the bend!'
   'Really, why's that?'
   'Because I love sausages.'
   'Nothing strange about that. I'm very fond of sausages myself.'
   'Really? You must come round some time and see my collection. I've got thousands.'

'Doctor, Doctor, I've got this terrible inferiority complex. I keep thinking people are ignoring me!'
   'Next patient, please . . .'

November 14th

Happy Birthday to Prince Charles (1948). When his son was born, Charles emerged from the maternity ward and declared: 'He's wonderful. And I'm like every other parent; I want my son to have all the things I couldn't have as a child . . . like India . . .'

Good old Aunty BBC began the first daily broadcasting service on this day in 1922. The original Beeb boss, Lord Reith, was such a stickler for properness that he insisted his announcers sho~ wear dinner-jackets when reading the news . . . on radio!

And do you know the origin of the pet-name for the ~ Beeb'? It was a phrase first coined by Yours Trul~

November 15th

Uncle Ken's Agony Column

Dear Uncle Ken...

I am a test pilot for the Royal Air Force. Recently, my Commanding Officer has told me he's not sure I'm quite as sharp as I used to be. This arose from an incident when, on a test-flight last week, I was asked by Air Traffic Control to state my height and position. Naturally I replied: 'I'm six-foot-two, and sitting in the cockpit.' Now my fellow pilots are laughing at me and calling me names like 'dingbat' and 'wimp'. I feel as though my career is over. My question is this: what's the best way of getting out of this tricky situation?

Uncle Ken writes:

One highly effective method of leaving such embarrassing situations behind is to stand in the fast lane of the motorway. There are several others which I can send you on receipt of a cheque for £50,000 made out to the Uncle Ken Foundation for People Who Shouldn't Be So Gullible As To Confide Their Problems In Agony Columnists.

November 16th

Many Happy Returns of the day to 50% of one of Britain's best comedy teams, Griff Rhys-Jones, who first saw the light of day in 1953.

And congratulations to Haven High School of Kansas who thrashed opponents Sylvia High School on this day in 1927. Nothing spectacular about that, you may think . . . but the score was 256–0!

I expect they'll be celebrating with a bottle of bubbly or two, but did you know that the record for the farthest-flying champagne cork is 105 feet and 9 inches?

November 17th

Many Happy Returns of the day to Peter Cook (1937). A savage wit (when he's in the mood), Peter can put down posers with the best of them. His neighbour at a dinner party told him she was writing a book. 'Neither am I,' replied the acid-tongued Cook.

THE KENNY EVERETT GUIDE TO SURVIVAL IN THE TWENTIETH CENTURY

(Culinary section)
When making shepherd's pie, try to avoid using real shepherds.

November 18th

Don't be taken by surprise this week. Find out what the stars have in store, thanks to Cuddly Ken's forecasting service. This week's SuperStar is

≈≈ AQUARIUS ♉

An unexpected challenge to your authority may surprise you, but not as much as the discovery that your left buttock is currently the star exhibit at the National Gallery. Your lucky number is 22,458,921½. Funnily enough, this number doesn't feature all that often in everyday life and may go some way towards explaining your recent run of bad luck.

November 19th

On this day in 1863 President Lincoln delivered the Gettysburg Address. Unfortunately, he delivered it to the wrong house and it languished for years among a pile of special offers from *Reader's Digest*.

Bathroom Brain-teasers

1 Which girl's name was invented by J.M. Barrie, author of Peter Pan?
2 How many igs in an ogg?
3 What happens after a Badedas bath?
4 If you are of average weight, how much fat could you expect to lose after walking for 24 hours?
5 What is the end of this joke?
    Knock Knock
    Who's there?
    Wendy
    Wendy who?

(Answers at foot of page)

November 20th

On this day in 1947 there was a right Royal hitch-up as the Queen married Prince Philip. Proving that there *is* a sense of humour there somewhere, she told a party of people gathered to celebrate her Silver Wedding: 'I think that everyone will concede that – today of all days – I should begin by saying "My husband and I . . .".'

Brain-teaser Answers

1) Wendy. 2) More than you'd expect. 3) Things. 4) One pound. 5) Wendy red red robin comes bob bob bobbin' along . . .

November 21st

Happy Birthday to Goldie Hawn (1945) and Harpo Marx (1888–1964). As Harpo hardly ever opened his mouth, it's not too surprising that none of his *bons mots* live on. Brother Chico, however, was once caught by his wife in the middle of kissing a chorus girl:

'I wasn't kissing her,' he said quickly, 'I was whispering in her mouth.'

Today's Loo Laff

Quiz questions:

Q: If all the cars in Britain were red, what would you have?
A: A red car-nation.

Q: Why do bears have fur coats?
A: They'd look silly in plastic macs.

Q: What do you call an eskimo's house with no lavatory?
A: An ig.

Q: How do you make a cigarette lighter?
A: Take the tobacco out.

November 22nd

Happy Birthday to Python Person Terry Gilliam (1940).

Helpful Household Hints (Part 36 of a 12-part series):
1 A silver spoon inserted in the neck of a half-finished bottle of champagne will keep the fizz fizzing.
2 A silver knife inserted in the neck of the *au pair* will ensure the swift arrival of the police.
3 If you have an aquarium, it is inadvisable to mix goldfish with members of the shark family.
4 It is inadvisable to mix gin with Marmite (except in months with an 'R' in them).

November 23rd

Astro-loogical personality profile for all those born under the sign of

SAGITTARIUS

(November 23rd –
December 21st):
The great bane of all Sagittarians' lives is their inability to make the right decision, and the difficulty they have in pronouncing the word 'putrify'. They admire strength of character in others, mainly because they possess none themselves. Many Sagittarians have a lisp, except the ones who don't. Their lucky day of the week is Jeremy.

November 24th

Happy Birthday to Ian Botham (1955) and The Big Yin, Billy Connolly (1942) who described fame as 'being asked to sign your name on the back of a fag packet'.

And fellow comedian Fred Allen once defined a celebrity as 'a person who works hard all his life to become well-known, then wears dark glasses to avoid being recognised'.

November 25th

Crystal ball time again, darling reader, and this week's SuperStar forecast is for

SAGITTARIUS

You will undergo a sudden religious conversion and join an obscure cult whose members worship deep-pile carpets. Your friends may not be entirely sympathetic to this newfound fervour, and you will find it rather hard to get converts. (I must apologise for a typographic error in the last forecast for Sagittarius: the sentence should read '*kiss* your mother', and not 'kill your mother'. May I take this opportunity to express my condolences.)

Happy Birthday to Tina Turner (1941), the only rock singer in the world whose legs go all the way up to her armpits.

November 26th

AMNESIACS CORNER
'There are three things I always forget: names, faces and . . . I can't remember the other.' (Italo Svevo)

QUOTES QUIZ:
The following sayings are often misquoted. What should the correct versions be?
a) 'Play it Again, Sam.'
b) 'I must warn you that anything you say may be taken down and used in evidence against you.'
c) 'Peace In Our Time.'

ANSWERS: *a)* Ingrid Bergman said, 'Play it once, Sam, for old time's sake,' and Humphrey Bogart said, 'If she can stand it, I can. Play it.'   *b)* The correct usage is, 'You are not obliged to say anything unless you wish to do so, but what you say may be put in writing and given in evidence.'   *c)* The actual phrase used by Neville Chamberlain was 'Put the kettle on, Mildred. I'm parched.'

November 27th

Happy Birthday to Ernie Wise (1915) and to Jimi Hendrix who's probably in a Purple Haze somewhere on a cloud.

THE WEARY WAITER:

Waiter, waiter! This egg's rotten.
Don't blame me sir, I only lay the tables.

Waiter, waiter! This plate is damp.
Yes, sir, that's the soup.

Waiter, waiter! Is this a dead spider in my soup?
I expect so sir, it's the heat that kills them.

November 28th

Bathroom Brain-teasers

1 Which future Queen of England said: 'I am as thick as a plank?' (NB – there is a clue contained in the question . . .)
2 What do you call a man wearing ear-muffs?
3 What is dwyle-flonking?
4 Which number gives you the same answer whether you add six to it, or multiply it by six?
5 What is bought by the yard and worn by the foot?

(Answers at foot of page)

PHILOSOPHICAL STATEMENT OF THE DAY
'Nothing is more irritating than not being asked to a party you wouldn't be seen dead at.'

Brain-teaser Answers
1) Yes, you're right; it was Princess Diana.   2) Anything you like – he can't hear you.   3) The flinging of wellington boots. He who throws furthest wins, and is extremely silly.   4) 1.2.   5) Carpet.

November 29th

Today's Loo Laff

Proudly presenting The World's Most Infuriating Knock-Knock Joke:

Knock knock
Who's there?
Granny
Granny who?
Knock knock
Who's there?
Granny
Granny who?
Knock knock
Who's there?
Granny
Granny who?
Knock knock
Who's there?
Auntie
Auntie who?
Aunt you glad Granny's gone?

November 30th

Winston Churchill was born today in 1874 and, as well as being remembered for all his 'blood, toil, tears and sweat', he had a few good one-liners up his sleeve, like the time when Bessie Braddock said to him, 'Winston, you're drunk!' And Churchill replied, 'Bessie, you're ugly. But tomorrow I shall be sober.'

Or his witty riposte when Lady Astor snarled, 'If you were my husband, I'd poison your coffee.' Churchill said, 'If you were my wife, I'd drink it.'

December 1st

Happy Birthday to three of the funniest people alive (not including Edwina Currie): Bette Midler (1945), Richard Pryor (1940) and the wonderful Woody Allen (1935). Did you know Woody's real name is Allen Konigsberg? Neither did I.

Woody on sex: 'Sex between a man and a woman can be wonderful – provided you get between the right man and the right woman.'

Woody on love: 'Love is the answer, but while you're waiting for the answer, sex raises some pretty good questions.'

Woody on religion: 'Not only is there no God, but try getting a plumber on weekends.'

December 2nd

This week's almost-not-too-bad-really-all-things-considered **Astro-loogical Forecast** is for

℔ ♈ **ARIES** ♎ ♏

Christmas shopping is likely to be stressful this week, but not nearly as stressful as lots of other things – like being sold to a slave-trader, or balancing a pile of camel-dung on the tip of your nose. Your lucky defrocked priest is Father Ignatius O'Hanrahan of Pease Pottage.

December 3rd

THE
KENNY EVERETT
GUIDE TO SURVIVAL IN THE
TWENTIETH CENTURY

If you want to keep your best friend, never make improper advances towards his aspidistra, and never chew off his right thumb.

Happy Birthday to Mel Smith (1952).

Bathroom Brain-teasers

Who wrote the following books . . .
1 *Hollywood Wives.*
2 *My Golden Wedding.*
3 *Let us Pray.*
4 *Crime Does Not Pay.*
5 *Sadness and Sorrow.*

(Answers at foot of page)

December 4th

Many Happy Returns of the day to three clever comics, Ronnie Corbett, Jimmy Jewel and Pamela Stephenson.

Today's Loo Laff

The canoodling couple were sitting on the sofa when Billy reached into his pocket and pulled out a small box which contained the tiniest diamond ring in the world. He placed it on Jenny's finger.

'Jenny . . . I know I'm not much of a catch. I know I don't have a flashy car, or a big house, or much money, or a yacht in the South of France, like my friend Harry does. But I truly love you.'

'Oh, Billy,' sighed Jenny. 'I love you too. But tell me more about your friend Harry . . .'

Brain-teaser Answers

1) Jackie Collins. 2) Annie Versary. 3) Neil Downe. 4) Laura Norder. 5) Anne Guish.

December 5th

Happy Birthday and a thousand thanks to Walt Disney (1901–1966) for all his fabbo movies. By all accounts, he went a bit batty in later life. 'Girls bored me,' he once said. 'They still do. I love Mickey Mouse more than any woman I've ever known.'

Other Potty Personages include Karen Stevenson of Merseyside – using a cocktail stick, she once ate 2,780 baked beans in 30 minutes – and Norman Johnson of Blackpool who, for reasons best known to himself, set a record for cucumber slicing: 244 slices in 13.4 seconds!

December 6th

PERSONALITY POSERS:

1 In an examination hall, you have the opportunity to peek at someone else's answers. Do you *a*) peek at someone else's answers, or *b*) remove both your eyeballs and juggle them in the air?

2 While making carrot-juice in a liquidiser, you accidentally liquidise your neighbour's poodle. Do you *a*) immediately put your house up for sale, or *b*) make a poodle-and-carrot-juice cocktail?

December 7th

MATTERS ORIENTAL

Today's the anniversary of the day when Pearl Harbor was attacked by the Japanese at 7.44 am, 1941.

More importantly, it's the day when we commemorate the day in 1911 which saw the outlawing of pigtails in China.

PHILOSOPHICAL STATEMENT OF THE DAY

Never get into a fight with ugly people because they have nothing to lose.

December 8th

American humorist James Thurber was born in 1894. In *Thurber Country* he wrote, 'A man should not insult his wife publicly, at parties. He should insult her in the privacy of the home.'

And I think he might have been a bit on the cynical side too: 'Let the meek inherit the earth – they have it coming to them.'

December 9th

Time for another peek-preview of what the fickle finger of fate has in store for you this week, and it's the turn of all those born under the sign of

≈AQUARIUS ♉

Being a romantic type of person, you seldom need any excuse to indulge in your passion for impersonating mushrooms. There is a chance that you may become the first person for many years to invent a new letter of the alphabet. If in doubt, knit one, purl two and turn left at the second set of traffic lights.

Many Happy Returns of the day to 'Coronation Street' which started on this day in 1960. (Did you know that the programme was originally to have been called 'Florizel Street'?)

December 10th

Helpful Household Hints (Part 12 of a 3-part series)
1 When friends arrive unexpectedly for dinner, either whip up some *doigts de poisson,* or lock yourself in the bread-bin.
2 Do not attempt to eat peas with a fork.
3 Do not attempt to eat spaghetti hoops through your nose.
4 If you run out of silver polish, throw all your silver away and buy a new set from Harrods.
5 If you throw away all your silver, please throw it at me.

December 11th

Bathroom Brain-teasers

1 Name the half of Wham! that wasn't George Michael.
2 Why does George Michael always sleep alone?
3 Where does the expression 'peeping Tom' come from?
4 How many slices of lemon cheesecake will it take to fill a Ford Transit van?
5 What is the telephone number of Buckingham Palace?

(Answers at foot of page)

Happy Birthday to squillionairess, Christina Onassis (1950). From all accounts, she's not the world's happiest woman but – as Woody Allen said – 'money is better than poverty, if only for financial reasons'.

December 12th

Happy Birthday to Ol' Blue Eyes, Frank Sinatra (1915).

Brain-teaser Answers

1) Andrew Ridgeley. 2) Because there isn't room for two on a sunbed. 3) Tom the Tailor who snook a glance at Lady Godiva when she rode naked through the streets of Coventry. 4) Lots. 5) 01 939 4832. (And do you know what the switchboard operator at the Palace says when she connects the Queen Mum for a natter with the Queen . . . 'Your Majesty? Her Majesty, Your Majesty . . .'

Today's Loo Laff

A filthy old tramp was playing his mouth-organ outside Harrods. On the pavement in front of him lay his shabby cap.

A very grand lady wafted out of the store, her arms filled with gift-wrapped packages.

'Excuse me, lady,' said the tramp. 'Can you spare fifty pence for a cup of tea?'

'Certainly not,' she sniffed.

'Well,' persevered the tramp. 'Perhaps you could spare me twenty pence . . .?'

'I've told you before, no!' said the lady frostily.

'Blimey,' said the tramp, 'you'd better take my mouth-organ. You're worse off than I am!'

December 13th

Many Happy Returns to comedian Jim 'nick-nick' Davidson (1954). Jim observed recently that today it's the young girls who sow their wild oats all night . . . and in the morning they pray for a crop failure.

Apparently he comes from a very poor family: 'so poor, in fact, that my brother was made in Hong Kong.'

And I like Jim's story about the little boy who went back to school after three days' absence. His teacher asked him why he had been away, and the little boy said, 'My dad was burnt.'

'Oh,' said the teacher, 'not seriously I hope.'

'Well,' he said, 'they don't mess about down at the crematorium, you know!'

December 14th

George Washington popped his clogs on this day in 1799 and – I'm sorry to disillusion you – the story about him never telling a lie is a load of old tosh.

You remember learning how he admitted cutting down his father's cherry tree, saying, 'Father – it was me. I cannot tell a lie. I am a very naughty future President.' Well, the tale was invented by his biographer, Mason Weems.

December 15th

FAIRLY FASCINATING FACT ABOUT EMPEROR NERO

Emperor Nero was born on this day in AD 37 – and stand by for another historical myth to be exploded. Information has come into my hands that Nero did not fiddle while Rome burned. How do I know this? Because the violin wasn't invented in those days! I rest my case.

DAFT DEFINITIONS

Cloak – the mating call of a Chinese frog.
Vice versa – dirty poems.
Coq-au-vin – love in a lorry.

December 16th

Happy Birthday to 'The Master' Noël Coward (1899–1973). My all-time favourite Nöel Coward story concerns the time when he was watching the 1953 Coronation on TV. Asked who was the man riding in a carriage with the overweight Queen of Tonga, Coward replied, 'Her lunch.'

Star-time once again, and there's an exciting time ahead for you if you're born under the sign of

You may now be entering a restless period in your life, or you may be entering the Hyde Park Underpass.

It's hard to tell from here, but not nearly as hard as tearing off a strip of cling-film without lacerating your fingers. Try to remember the wise words of Our Lady of the Daffodils: 'The secret of staying young is to live honestly, eat sensibly, and lie about your age.'

December 17th

Uncle Ken's Agony Column

Dear Uncle Ken...

I am writing because I hate going to school. All the teachers laugh at me, I hate playing games, I hate lessons, and I'm teased mercilessly by every boy and girl in the whole place. I asked my Mum if I had to carry on going to school, and she said 'Yes'. As I'm the headmaster, I suppose she has a point.

My ambition is to be a big-game hunter but I need some advice about wild animals, and my question is this: where do you find wild elephants?

Uncle Ken writes:

That depends on where you leave them.

December 18th

POTTY PLAYWRIGHT
J. R. Ronden wrote a play called *The Play Without An A* which was performed for the first and last time on this day in 1816. For reasons best known to Ronden (and his psychiatrist), there was not a single word in the play which contained the letter A.

(Maybe I'm a simple old sausage, but what exactly is wrong with the letter A? Answers on a postcard please.)

THE KENNY EVERETT GUIDE TO SURVIVAL IN THE TWENTIETH CENTURY

Never try to swallow a whole Axminster carpet at one go. Always dice it into fine slices first.

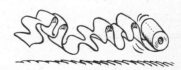

December 19th

Bathroom Brain-teasers

1 What does the name Peter mean?
2 What do you call an Underground train full of University professors?
3 Which letter begins English words most often?
4 What is the favourite snack of the female mosquito?
5 What was Elvis Presley's middle name?

(Answers at foot of page)

Happy Birthday to dear old Sir Ralph Richardson (1902–1983) who once said: 'The art of acting consists in keeping people from coughing.'

December 20th

Happy Birthday to Bo Derek (1957). Not widely respected for her acting abilities, a critic once wrote of the luscious Bo: 'Her performance was so wooden that she ought to be investigated for dry rot.'

Today's Loo Laff

Two little boys were watching a video of *Bolero* starring Bo Derek.

'You know what?' said one of the boys. 'If I ever stop hating girls, I think I'll stop hating Bo Derek first.'

Brain-teaser Answers

1) Rock. 2) A tube of Smarties. 3) 'S'. 4) Blood. 5) Aaron.

December 21st

Happy Birthday to Tory Prime Minister Benjamin Disraeli, born today in 1804. Like many politicians, Disraeli enjoyed scoring points off his opponents – especially William Gladstone. Once, when asked what was the difference between a calamity and a misfortune, Disraeli replied, 'If Gladstone fell into the Thames it would be a misfortune, but if someone pulled him out again it would be a calamity.'

December 22nd

Astro-loogical personality profile for all those born under the sign of

CAPRICORN

(December 22nd –
January 20th):
Capricorn-esque people are the salt of the earth. Sweet-natured, eager to please others, easy-going and generous to a fault. Many Capricornians are small but perfectly formed, bearded, slightly daft and have their own hugely successful series on BBC television. They make great lovers, superb disc-jockeys and wonderful *spaghetti alle vongole*.

Their one drawback is that they constantly hide their light under a bushel and then have great difficulty retrieving it. (By the way, I'm a Capricorn too.)

December 23rd

SuperStar time again, ladies and gentlephones, and this week's Zodiac is a right mix-up I can tell you: Mars is currently moving into Jupiter, which means Jupiter's getting pretty overcrowded and is thinking of buying a bungalow by the sea with easy access to the shops. In the meantime, this week's **Astro-loogical Forecast** is for

You will be the focus of attention all over the world this week when you become the first person to invent a digital gherkin. You should be aware, however, that there is little demand for digital gherkins. In these dark and dangerous days, remember: never mispronounce the word 'chamberpot' and never trust a man with a lettuce-leaf growing behind his ear.

December 24th

According to an ancient legend, if a young woman bakes a loaf of bread on Christmas Eve, she will know the identity of her husband-to-be. All she has to do is score her initials on the loaf and leave it by the fire before going to bed. As the clock strikes twelve, the spitting image of her future fiancé will appear out of nowhere, write his initials next to the girl's and vanish into thin air.

THE
KENNY EVERETT
GUIDE TO SURVIVAL IN THE
TWENTIETH CENTURY

Never believe daft old legends about baking cakes on Christmas Eve.

December 25th

Many Happy Returns of the day to the lovely Me.

According to another old legend (one which I find much more credible), any child born on this day is supposed to be absolutely oozing with genius and psychic powers!

Before you stuff the crackers and pull the turkey, spare a thought for Danish Dingbat Anders Jensen who predicted that the world would end on this day in 1967. Along with fifty other Danish Dimwits, he spent Christmas Day in a fall-out shelter and was extremely annoyed to find that he was wrong!

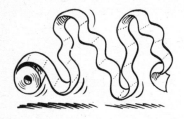

December 26th

Happy Birthday to Mao-Tse Tung (1893–1976). Among Mao's famous sayings is, 'The longest journey begins with a single step.' Among Mao's lesser-known sayings are:

1 When going on a long journey, a good way of saving space in the suitcase is to stuff your socks into your shoes.'
2 'It is better to travel hopefully than to travel with a piece of sticky toffee wedged between your teeth.'

December 27th

Happy Birthday to Marlene Dietrich (1904) who observed wryly, 'Most women set out to try to change a man, and when they have changed him they do not like him.'

Bathroom Brain-teasers

1 What is Sting's real name?
2 What was Question One in this section of Brain-teasers?
3 Which pop star's real name is Gordon Sumner?
4 What is the next question in this section of Brain-teasers?
5 Who was the lead singer with The Police?

(Answers at foot of page)

December 28th

Today's Loo Laff

Out of the mouths of babes . . .

'Mum, you know that Ming vase? The one that's been handed down from generation to generation?
'Yes, what about it?'
'Well, this generation's dropped it.'

A friend told me about the time he took his six-year-old twins to the circus. Afterwards, they were discussing the thrills and spills they'd seen under the Big Top. One of the twins said, 'I didn't think much of the knife-thrower. He kept on chucking knives at that soppy girl in sequins, and he didn't hit her once!'

Brain-teaser Answers

1) Gordon Sumner.   2) What is Sting's real name?   3) Sting.
4) Who was the lead singer with The Police?   5) Sting.

December 29th

PERSONALITY POSERS:

1 Your Mum gave you a Christmas present which is unique in its hideousness. Do you *a*) change the present, or *b*) change your Mum?

2 You discover that your grandmother has knees which, over the years, have transformed into solid mahogany. Do you *a*) commiserate with her misfortune, or *b*) make the most of the situation and use her as a bedside chest?

December 30th

The final SuperStar Forecast of the year, and it's for all those born under the sign of

CAPRICORN

Never let it be said that you're a mean-spirited old wombat, nor that you don't always do your very best to be kind to 'J-Cloths'. Now that your plan to laminate Meryl Streep has fallen through, you can devote more time to your collection of Renaissance ear-wax. In the meantime, I shall be very happy to accept your apologies, and I promise to keep them somewhere safe until next time you need them.

December 31st

In Austria they celebrate New Year's Eve by Touching a Pig For Luck.

Suggested New Year Resolutions:

1 Resolve to avoid spending New Year's Eve in Austria.
2 Resolve to give up everything you enjoy that's really bad for you.
3 Resolve to put off making any resolutions until next year.
4 Resolve to always carry some olive oil with you – in case you come across an olive that needs oiling!